THE LIVING BREATH OF CORNWALL

By the same author:

Voyage into Cornwall's Past
From Rock and Tempest
The Inconstant Sea
Facing the Sea
The Story of Glendorgal
The Printer and his Offspring
The Newspaper in Cornwall, 18th-19th Centuries
The House on the Seine
Teach Yourself to Fly
Britain in the Air
Red, White and Spain
The Air is our Concern

THE LIVING BREATH OF CORNWALL

NIGEL TANGYE

WILLIAM KIMBER · LONDON

First published in 1980 by
WILLIAM KIMBER & CO. LIMITED
Godolphin House, 22a Queen Anne's Gate,
London, SW1H 9AE

© Nigel Tangye, 1980
ISBN 0 7183 0008 4

This book is copyright. No part of it may be reproduced in any form without permission in writing from the publishers except by a reviewer who wishes to quote brief passages in connection with a review written for inclusion in a newspaper, magazine, radio or television broadcast.

© *Poem opposite,* A. L. Kimber 1980

Typeset by Granada Typesetting
Redhill
and printed and bound in Great Britain by
Redwood Burn Limited,
Trowbridge and Esher

Cornwall – that strange primordial piece of land
Flung into brilliant light and binding blue
And clinging mists, and all the dangers and delights
Of unpredictable deep seas, that give and take away
With ruthless and beguiling ease.

The living breath of your strong sons, long dead,
Still finds itself in lash of purifying spray.
The blowing whiteness of the foam above stark ringing rocks,
And sighs, perhaps, across quiet fields and places steep
They knew as home.

A.L.K.

Contents

		Page
	Acknowledgements	10
	Introduction	11
I	Setting the Scene	13
II	My Lords Impetuous, of Boconnoc	20
III	The Saint in Golden, Cuthbert Mayne	56
IV	Mr Flindell and Mr Heard	76
V	The Young Tangye Brothers of Illogan	100
VI	The Singular Richard Lander	129
VII	John Harris: The Miner, the Heart and the Song	158
	Appendix	169
	Bibliography	170
	Index	173

A map of Spray's voyage appears on pages 50-51.

Acknowledgements

For their help in providing me with search material I would like to offer my thanks to the following: Miss Joan Bailey, London Library, to Miss Angela Broome, Assistant Librarian at the Royal Institution of Cornwall, to Mr David Ivall, Cornwall County Record Office, to Mr D. Knight, Librarian, County Local History Library, Redruth; and to Mr R.D. Penhallurick, Assistant Curator, Truro Museum, for his delightful map.

I am also grateful to Mrs D. Burnie, for kindly allowing me to reproduce Richard Lander's letter to William IV, and to Mr P. L. Hull, County Archivist, for releasing it.

N.T.

Introduction

I tilt this book toward the ever-growing number of people who are interested in the story of Cornwall but who do not feel equipped enough to delve into conventional history books.

In particular, I write it to help expand the horizon of those of us who are more and more seeking, unconsciously, assurance from archaeology, historical records, artefacts, biographies, even vintage car clubs as a counter to our anxiety regarding the future and the onrush of technology.

This ever-widening interest, this groping into the past by ordinary people who would by no stretch of the imagination call themselves historians, is encouraged by the comfort of being persuaded that each of us is a particle in the stream of history, whose momentum drives through the present and into the future. This identification as human beings with those in past generations, men and women, with ills and joys and foibles like ourselves, gives us a satisfying sense of belonging, which itself brings its own brand of security.

This new sense of belonging is vividly felt by anyone who, never having looked further back than his grandparents, suddenly finds through modest family history research, that he is of a proven line going back several generations. From then on, he feels a bigger, a more confident person.

And so it is that in pursuit of the foregoing thesis, I withdraw from their environment of time and space those who have provided the weft and the warp of the Cornish tapestry, and I present them as individuals to my readers who might not otherwise meet them.

To effect this, I invite the reader on board my sailing ketch, *Spray*, to share my experience as she cruises down the long line of high cliffs of North Cornwall. Here is the face of Cornwall displaying its character in serried surface and varied colour, conveying the story of the lively people behind it, while *Spray* sails on down towards Land's End.

I
Setting the Scene

One afternoon in early summer I was visiting the strange complex of spectacular, jumbled rock and vegetation of Hartland Point. Hither the tough, arrogant Cornish coast strides up from Land's End, meeting the gentle boundary of Devon a few miles to the south while the great cliffs continue northward. On reaching this graphic cornerstone of Hartland where the Atlantic hands over to the Bristol Channel, the Severn Sea as it used to be called, the cliffs refine and diminish into the easier life implied by gentle names like Clovelly, Bideford, Appledore.

It was while I was standing on the cliff edge by the coastguards' wide-windowed hut that the idea of viewing the history of my county from the sea came to me.

Far down below the sea was lazily running up and along a plateau of serrated rock of murderously savage character that even the placid incoming waves could not conceal as being anything else. The rock was formed in narrow parallel ribs, as individual in their fashioning as the venerable pillar rocks of Land's End. Seaward, beyond the smooth expanse of blue sea, looking to me as precisely the same as it looked to an onlooker ten thousand years ago, a million years perhaps, lay the horizon, not a sharp line this afternoon but a soft finale to the smooth blue sea.

I was pondering on the strange property of the sea that gives it a unique quality in terms of time. I look at the cliffs stretching north and south, and the landscape behind me, and I know that time brings with it erosion and decay, so that neither permits me to share with past generations precisely the visual experience of seeing what they saw.

Not so the sea. The sea is unchanging. The winds may ruffle

it, rumple it, torment it, but the sea responds in exactly the same way as it always has throughout history.

The seaman today views it as did the seaman of yesterday, and as did the first of our race in times of pre-history.

Dwelling on this immensely exciting thought, that there *is* such a thing as a visual link spanning the ages, between ourselves and primitive man and all generations between, I looked down from my cliff top and my attention was back in the present. Slowly approaching from the north on the silent blue sea far below there was a white yacht, like a resting seabird.

She was sailing toward Cornwall, southward, and she had her spinnaker up, rotund and white like the breast of a well-fed, satiated gull on the water, smoothly paddling. With wind astern she glided slowly along her path, a divine picture of contentment, a boat in her element on a lovely day.

I wondered if those on board this leisure craft would do more than glance at the phalanx of cliffs on this calm day, and if they would see in their geological face the character of Cornwall, from the rugged stubbornness of rock defying the assault of wind and sea, to the kindliness of the pasture and flowers in the winding combes that shape the path of stream to ocean. And I wondered if those on board felt the presence of their fellow seamen in storm and tempest in these waters over the centuries, their spirits lingering in the countless tangled wrecks that line the cliff foot from Hartland Point to Land's End.

The white yacht had no fears. She was by now but a small speck on the calm sea, and I envied those on board cruising down this historic coast so serenely, with the opportunity presented them to sense, or to read, or to ponder as they passed, the history inland from the great cliff; from beyond the sand-washed estuary, and within the unsheltered bay.

It was two years later that I found myself in my 30-foot ketch, *Spray*, turning south off Hartland Point, following in the wake of that white seabird, and receptive to the voice of Cornish history in the sound of gulls, the swish of spray, and thunder of tumbling waves.

Cruising down the north coast in *Spray*, I allowed my thoughts to wander. Sometimes the great cliffs, or the yellow beach, sent a message to me, a call to the past, and I would wonder what circumstance, what event, in the past might be the trigger that set my mind turning with the revolving wheel of history. Soon I would relate, quite clearly, to someone or something that had a clue for me planted amongst the serried surfaces of those legendary loquacious cliffs.

The notes I made while *Spray* sailed down the first stretch of coast were published under the title *Voyage into Cornwall's Past*. In this we had several companions from out of the story of Cornwall. These included Sir Bevill Grenville of Stowe, Thomasine Bonaventura who became Lady Mayoress of London, Sir Richard Grenville of the *Revenge*, Lawrence Braddon and the Tower of London. Also there joined us the two romantic, adventurous poets, Lord Byron and Shelley, and, too, the astonishing adventurer Edward Trelawny, who captivated among many others the Drury Lane actress Fanny Kemble. More surprising, perhaps, was the poignant story of Thomas Hardy and the girl from the St Juliot vicarage.

I am now going to take up once more the story of this voyage into the past with *Spray* and I rejoice to feel myself on board her again.

We are at sea just south of Boscastle, having spent the night 'lying to' some three miles off the coast, and now I am heading south again. I wholly identify myself with all the seamen who have preceded me in these waters. To be alone at sea at night is as if you were on a bridge that spans time, or rather defuses it so that the experience is precisely the same as it was by those in ages past. The reason for this is that nothing is changed, as I have already mentioned, but more positively there is the experience, heightened at night at sea, of the unchanged message to eye and ear, the dark velvet of night and the glow of starlight on the restless water, the haphazard splashes of water against the hull, the soft zephyrs of air on the cheek. All this I share with the seamen of the ages. From it I draw, like they did, the warmth of continuity and comradeship; and the humility from being in the presence of God.

I have little idea how the spirit is going to move me, what names in the story of Cornwall will be spelt out to me by the language of the coastline, by the song of the gulls, from the infinite variety of mood and balance between wind and sea.

On this grey morning, when the sea and sky share a gradation of greys and little colour, the magnificent cliffs of varied slopes and shapes are, from this distance of two miles, but a dark line of monochrome dividing sea from sky. But then soon emerges the distinctive, massive feature of the Tintagel Isthmus, focusing my attention away from the anonymity of the sea and on to one of the great historical mysteries in our story, the place in it of King Arthur and his famous knights. For me, in fact, it is a myth soured by commercial exploitation to a quite unacceptable degree of vulgar triviality, and though I deeply respect the mystery of its substance, and the honest labours of scholars from many lands and periods to establish its source, I cannot dispel a compelling desire to yawn whenever good King Arthur and his knights approach.

The legend attached to Tintagel that I much prefer is the romantic story of Tristan and Isolde who fall in love when Tristan goes to fetch Isolde as the bride of his uncle, King Mark, whose castle was Tintagel. There are many versions of this tragic story emanating from different countries in Europe, and every one suggests, if not defines, the setting to be Cornwall. And how divinely linked to Tintagel is Wagner's exquisite opera about this fateful romance.

The situation and remains of the castle itself provide enough food for romanticism for the visitor without embellishment from a myth. Indeed, its resistance to the onslaught of archaeologists and historians over the ages, and its refusal to provide any real evidence as to its history, are enough to arouse a very special curiosity, and one that repays even the faint-hearted to tackle the walk up to it.

Today, this path to the castle is well eased for the visitor by the steps, and the bridge across the isthmus, but it still requires, nevertheless, lots of breath and respect. Read now what Norden wrote of this very same path as it was about 1580. John Norden was a topographer who made the first map of Cornwall, and should you visit Tintagel your experience will be enriched by reminding yourself of how one man found that same approach four hundred years ago:

> The principal buylding seemeth to be on the mainland, from whence a Draw-bridge was let downe to pass to the Ilande to the other buyldings; but of late yeares, within man's memorie, it is depryved of the benefit of a bridge, and the

passage to the Ilnade is nowe farr more irksome by a little Isthmos or neck of lande which lyeth at the foote of the rock of Ilande, the descent into it very steep and craggie, from whence the ascent againe is farr more tedious and daungerous, by a very narrow, rockye and wyndinge waye up the steep sea-cliffe . . . . for the least slipp of the foote sendes the whole bodye into the devouring sea; and the worst of all is higheste of all, nere the gate of entraunce into the hill, where the offensive stones so exposed, hange over the head, as while a man respecteth his footinge he indanngers his head . . . . but being once ascended and entred, ther is a very spatious greene Plot where Sheepe and Conyes feed. In the toppe of the Ilande is a fountayne and of sweete water, rising out of the mayne rock, which to consider is the more wounderfull, by how muche the Ilande is verie highe, and gyrte about with the mayne salte ocean . . . . . .

By now, after reading Norden, and being on the top of the 'Ilande', your footsteps will have joined, in mind, those of history; and when you turn to look at the splendour of the view out to sea, its proud, broad expanse stretching to the horizon, you can gain further magic, can put the inexorable onward discipline of Time in its place, and feel yourself alongside those of our forbears as they enjoyed exactly the same scene as you are viewing, thousands of years ago. It's quite a thought.

Tintagel promontory is now astern of us, and *Spray* and I are settled on course along the dramatic coastline some three miles off the general set of cliffs.

We are sailing free, running before the 10-knot wind, the white expanse of mainsail square on to me, telescoping my focus from free sea to the beautiful curves of the wind-filled canvas.

I luxuriate, on this warm day of early summer, in the languorous, luxurious motion of the boat playing its game with the smooth, crestless waves. There is an endless, unconfined symphony of movement, of curves and cushions, a ballet of playful balance. I share in the swish of the cleaved water as it passes, and I counter, with a touch on the tiller, the smack of the sail as the bow yaws, tentatively either side, in its playful contest with the tiller.

I am reclining in the cockpit, relishing the sense of solitude one has alone in a boat at sea, a solitude that is not wholly complete, for the shades of fellow seamen who have passed through aeons of time on this same track are never really far away.

I look at the high coastline slowly gliding by and contemplate how the survival of the fittest applies to the cliffs of Cornwall as much as anything else. Tough fists of coastline have been strong enough to withstand the onslaught of winter winds and seas but, as the less tough erode away, slowly in retreat, these remain in the form of promontories or headlands jutting out from the line of cliffs, now behind them. They have adapted their contours to minimise the power of the onslaught. As *Spray* moves down the coast she passes one of these every two or three miles.

Atop these green fingers jutting into the sea a streamline form had been assumed with curves where edges and planes are elsewhere. A gentle slope, fashioned unwittingly by the fury of the gales, wanders down toward its seaward extremity, and there it takes a sudden curve down to the vertical, ending with a bend seaward linking the underwater rocks with the face.

And most of the way down the coast, miraculously in face of the conditions, are these sloping promontories covered with vegetation, soft to the foot and easy to laze on. Indeed, the whole environment on a summer's day beguiles one into forgetting that down there are the ghosts of ships and men shattered on those black rocks at the foot of the cliffs, and this grim toll of death and destruction has by no means finished today, nor will it ever be.

Passing the tiny little havens of Port Isaac, Port Quin and Port Gaverne, we are in sight of the tall Day Mark on top of Stepper Point at the mouth of Camel Estuary on which lies Padstow. Its smiling face of sand-dunes, bathing beaches and blue smooth water, gives no hint, to the incoming ship, that this has been perhaps the most ravenous estuary for wrecks of any in the country. The reason for this is the Doom Bar, a bank of sand lurking unseen beneath the water, stretching the mile across and leaving only a narrow passage for ships right against the western arm. The lifeboats have, in their time, saved eight hundred lives and more, and in one terrible storm each of the two Padstow lifeboats on duty was lost on the same service.

The river Camel had very much a mind of its own. Its source

is near the northern boundary of the county at which several other streams begin their apprenticeship. But whereas these follow each other's lead and flow as rivers southwards, then bearing eastwards toward Tamar, the Camel after a few miles flicks its tail in the face of its colleagues, and turns smartly away from them and makes its way to the west coast at Padstow.

Perhaps its independent character has been induced by it being one of those many places I have referred to that lay some claim of participation in the Arthurian act. At all events the river passes through the quiet market town of Camelford, and it is to the bridge across the river that clings a legend that King Arthur met his death there, in the year AD 823, in a battle against his treacherous nephew Mordred. So says Camden. Carew, writing at the end of the sixteenth century, put the date of this legendary battle at AD 525 — so there you are, you can take your choice over this completely unimportant example of non-provenance.

However, notoriety, if not fame, *is* linked to the name of Camelford in a manner that earns it a place in history, albeit a minor place, but one that is spectacular, one that is peppered with the sparks from swords of duellists and the curl of pistol smoke in the cold morning air.

Lord Camelford, whose seat was never there but at Boconnoc, near Liskeard, drew widespread notoriety for his dashing, turbulent place in eighteenth century society, and it is he that is going to engage our wrapt attention now, as we follow his career until its violent end from a pistol shot in the Park at Kensington.

The lovely estate of Boconnoc plays its part in this story, and almost certainly had an influence on Lord Camelford's predilection for duelling. And why? For the reason that Camelford spent much of his boyhood alone in the big house, and who can doubt that he was not friendly with the ghost of a previous owner, Lord Mohun, who also was killed, after a stormy life, by a duellist's bullet in Kensington? But that was a century and a half earlier.

Boconnoc was the influence these two fiery gentlemen shared,and we shall meet each of them, striking individuals from well-known families and tied to a stern code of personal honour.

II

My Lords Impetuous, of Boconnoc

Some eight miles south-west of Liskeard, and a little to the south of Bradock Down, there lies a splendid mansion set graciously in a landscape of trees. Its handsome face has been demurely hidden by the trees for more than five centuries, and today, in this age of public access to stately homes, it is still as shy of its virtues as ever it was.

However, Boconnoc has played, at times, an important part in Cornish history, and at one time a vital part. Men with great names have dwelt there, kings have lodged there. Scandal has made other honoured names become notorious, like Mohun and Camelford, two of the succession of owners whose lively, impetuous conduct tarnished the legacy of talent and duty left by their forbears.

The story of Boconnoc is made the more fascinating by the fact that the manor is off the beaten track and remains as a private residence for the family of Fortescue, whose property it has been since the end of the eighteenth century. Not for this family the trauma, mixed with relief from the financial taskmaster of relentless upkeep, of handing their home over to the National Trust. For their sake long may that continue; for our sake I selfishly hope that one day its doors may be more widely opened.

For the present, then, I will give a description of Boconnoc by someone who was able to visit it and who accorded his impressions. As is my wont, I release at this point, and with no hard feelings, those rather faint-hearted readers who, perhaps impatient with description, seek only narrative, and I look forward to them rejoining me on page 22.

Our guide, to whom I have just referred, is Mr Samuel Drew,

of St Austell, who recorded what follows in his *History of Cornwall* published in 1824:

> The House, the seat of noble families, has at present the appearance of convenience rather than of magnificence. ... No traces of the ancient castellated mansion in which the Carminows and the Courtenays, and the ancient Mohuns, resided, are conspicuous, though it has been said that some portion of the ancient walls has been incorporated in the present building [Built early 18th century]......Another wing was added by the first Lord Camelford from his own design, and in this wing there is a gallery 110 feet long which opens into a drawing-room and library.
>
> The gallery and several of the apartments are ornamented with many elegant portraits among which are Sir Reginald Mohun and an old lady, believed to have been his grandmother, by Cornelius Jansen (1636), a finely executed portrait of Governor Pitt by Kneller, the Duchess of Cleveland by Sir Peter Lely, the Marquis of Buckingham by Sir Joshua Reynolds.... In the billiard room is a bust of the late Lord Camelford dating from 1790, and another of the great Earl of Chatham [William Pitt] by Wilson....
>
> Among the rare and curious furniture preserved in this splendid mansion, there is an antique cabinet of tortoise-shell inlaid with silver, representing the principal of Ovid's Metamorphoses: there is also a small table, and a pair of carved chairs of ebony, made out of the cradle of Queen Elizabeth. ...
>
> In the park are vestiges of some ancient lead-mines, one of which was worked in the reign of Charles I, and again in the year 1750; but it was not sufficiently productive in either case to defray the expense of the adventure.
>
> The adjacent grounds are varied and broken, and their beauty considerably enhanced by the woody scenery, and the retired [sic] vales with which they are ornamented. Through these vales run the tributary streams of a pellucid brook which, after bubbling through the groves that wave their foliage over the margins, form in their confluence the little river of Lerrin, which discharges itself in Fowey Harbour.

The time has now come when I can confidently suggest to my absent readers that they may now safely return, for from now on I shall be speaking of people and their odd doings to a background I have by now adequately, I hope, sketched.

Early ownership of Boconnoc, (the existence of which is recorded in Domesday book, 1087), is uncertain. The first owner we are fairly sure of, according to Lysons (1814), appears in the reign of Henry III as the family of De Cancia, or De Cant (c. 1268). Soon after it became the seat of the Carminows, and then of Sir Hugh Courtenay who settled at Boconnoc, and lost his life at the battle of Tewkesbury in 1471.

In all probability the estate then became vested in the Crown in consequence of an attainder in the Courtenay family. We then hear of it being in the hands of Lord Russell, and in 1579, the Earl of Bedford sold it to Willian Mohun, later Sir William Mohun, who died only eight years later. Nevertheless, Sir William Mohun creates a milestone in our story, for he had a son, Sir Reginald, and a grandson John who became, in 1628, Baron Mohun of Okehampton.

The Mohun family, was installed at Boconnoc at the time of the Civil War, and was at home to welcome Charles I when he crossed the Border into Cornwall to lead the Cornish troops against the Parliamentarians under the Earl of Essex.

Boconnoc in that summer of 1643 was the centre of the Royalist effort, an effort in which four separately raised Royalist Armies were united. The King was to stay until 4th September.

Sir Richard Grenville had just captured Bodmin, and when the King arrived at Boconnoc at the beginning of August, the Royalist line ran from Grampound to Bodmin and thence over the hills above Lostwithiel to Boconnoc some four miles away, and then on to Liskeard.

On 11th August 1644 the King unsuccessfully attempted a personal appeal to Essex to unite his army with the Royal one and so rejoin his country and the Crown, promising him, on the word of the King, eminent marks of his confidence and value. Essex turned this down flatly. A second appeal to Essex two days later was also rejected.

Lord Mohun was at the centre of things on the King's staff and no doubt shared the view of all concerned at this exciting time, that Essex with his back to the sea was on the point of defeat and was mad not to accept the King's generous offer. It was a near thing, and subsequent history would have been very different if the King had succeeded in his effort to prize Essex away from Cromwell, a move that could have led at that early stage in the War to Cromwell's defeat.

Five days before the King had arrived at Boconnoc, and while Lord Mohun was out with the Army, a curious episode occurred that might have ended with the capture of Essex. Drew describes it thus:

> On an adjacent hill from Boconnoc House are the remains of a square entrenchment called St Nighton's Beacon, which appears from the *Historical Discourses of Sir Edward Walker* to have been made by the troops of Charles I. It appears from the author who accompanied Charles on his expedition into Cornwall, and whose manuscript was corrected by the King's own hand, that Sir Bernard Gascoigne surprised and took possession of Boconnoc House in 4th August 1644, at which time it was garrisoned by some of the Parliamentary forces under the command of the Earl of Essex, several of whose officers, having met at this time to spend the day in festivity, were made prisoners.

Two years later, Lord Mohun was again to act as host to royalty, this time to the future sovereign, Charles II. There is in existence a warrant signed by Prince Charles from 'our Court at Boconnoc' for fishing in the river Lerrin. It is dated 10th November 1646.

In contrast to these turbulent times, is the irascible, contentious life-style of Charles Mohun, son of John, that I am about to relate, but first I offer the following gem of peaceful living and innocence experienced by one of the Mohuns of this period.

I take it from Lake's *Parochial History Vol I* (1867). Writing on the subject of the parish church of Boconnoc, he tells of the empty spaces on the walls from where the many tablets had been taken down and stored in the vaults below. A solitary one remaining bore the following inscription:

To the memory of the trewly vertuous Penelope, the daughter of Sir Reynold Mohun, Knight and Barronet, for a short time wife unto William Drew, of Broad Henbury, in the County of Devon, Esquire.

> My name was Mohun — my fate like various were;
> My short life's often changes maks it cleare,
> A virgin star on earth awhile I shined,
> With noted splendour, chiefly of the mind;
> Till my Will: Drew me to his nuptial bed,
> Thence soone by God's high call to heaven I fled,
> Not without hope in Christ to live agen,
> Set in the walls of new Jerusalem.
> *Who was buried the 30th day of March, 1633.*

By contrast, the historian, Tonkin, writing in 1737, summed up the life of Lord Charles Mohun, the last of the Mohuns of Boconnoc, thus:

> This Charles, Lord Mohun, was a nobleman of very bright parts, and great natural endowments, both of body and mind, but having had the misfortune of losing his father while he was yet in the cradle, and the estate being left to him much involved in lawsuits between his nearest relations, and with a considerable debt, he had not an education bestowed on him suitable to his birth; and happening to fall into company, he was drawn into several extravagancies.
>
> But, however, as his years increased, he became so much reclaimed as to give great hopes that he would one day equal the greatest of his predecessors, when he was thus unfortunately cut off in the flower of his age.
>
> He was twice married. First, to Charlotte, daughter of Thomas Manwaring, Esquire, by whom he had only one daughter whom he never owned, and he lived for several years separated from his wife. He had the good fortune, however to get rid of her at last, she being drowned in a passage to Ireland with one of her gallants, about six or seven years before his own death.
>
> Fitton Gerrard, Earl of Macclesfield, her maternal uncle, to make him some amends for this bad bargain, gave Charles, by will, a good part of his estate in 1701 which was

the occasion of the quarrel between his Lordship and the Duke of Hamilton, so fatal to them both.

Lord Charles Mohun lived in an era in which the duel, as the means of upholding one's honour in a dispute, was flourishing. This was in spite of the fact it took two to agree to a duel and that death to either challenger or challenged was more the rule than the exception. But refusal to answer a challenge, no matter how outrageously flippant the cause, emanating, perhaps, from a young blood in his cups, was made impossible because of the dishonour it brought to the helpless man challenged.

This custom brought spectacular gladiatorial opportunities for derring-do types of hot-blooded nature, who sought to gain acclaim from the ladies who, in one way or another, were often the cause of the quarrel now to be expurgated in blood. The brutality of the custom was disguised by the cloak of gracious ritual and deference.

This was a climate that such as Lord Charles Mohun could not find more welcome. His aggressive nature, his sense of the dramatic, his conceit and his innate lack of self-confidence in society, as a result of his lonely upbringing, all these combined to make him embrace the spectacular opportunities to display courage that the duel involved, and to waste no time picking quarrels which could lead to a solution by the sword or pistol.

Among the several duels that he fought was one with Lord Kennedy, but no other details are known as to the cause for this confrontation. More is known about one that he had in December 1694. A Mr Scobell, a Cornish MP, accosted Lord Mohun in Pall Mall to try and stop him apparently trying to kill a coachman who had displeased him in some way. Mohun was not unexpectedly livid at this intervention and with a scream of fury cut poor Mr Scobell over his head. This did not satisfy his lordship and he later challenged the MP who somehow got out of the unwelcome predicament.

The next occasion for which we have a record is his engaging in a duel with a Captain Bingham when he was wounded in the hand. More detail is known of his encounter with Captain Hill, of the Foot Guards, at Rummer Tavern on 14th September 1697. This ended in victory for Mohun and death for Captain Hill. Sir Bernard Burke, in his *Romance of the Aristocracy*, published in 1855, gives the detail from which, with generous help of Baring-Gould with the narrative, I extract what follows.

During the summer of 1697, a leading actress playing at the Theatre Royal, Drury Lane, was a Mrs Bracegirdle, hardly a name to conjure up allure or romance. However, Mrs B. was extremely popular having a singing voice that was both delicious and remarkable for its flexibility. And a critic writing of her rendering of Statira in a play about Alexander the Great was of the opinion that 'scarcely an audience saw her that were not half her lovers without a suspected favourite among them.' And then, lest he had gone too far, he made known that in an age of general dissoluteness she bore an immaculate reputation, and all the licentious men about town knew perfectly well that she was beyond the reach of their solicitations. But that did not prevent them trying, as we shall see. With Lord Charles Mohun in the wings, let the actors take the stage.

One of the actors playing at Drury Lane was a Mr Mountford, and his wife was a close friend of Mrs Bracegirdle, a friendship that gave rise to unkind assumptions, such as the belief that the only reason for this friendship was that Mrs B. was mad about this actor, and her frienship with his wife was no more than a ploy to see more of him.

This poor man soon found himself innocently in trouble, for a handsome officer of the Foot Guards, named Captain Richard Hill, was already infatuated with the actress and was determined to marry her. On proposing to her and being rejected he formed the conclusion that the actor Mountford, rival that he took him to be, had influenced Mrs B. in her decision.

At a supper party held shortly after this rebuff, Captain Hill swore to the assembled company that Mountford had been responsible for Mrs B.'s decision and accordingly must be killed, yes, killed. So far as Mrs B. was concerned, only he can have her. He would carry her off by force.

With Hill at the supper were Lord Mohun and Colonel Tredham, and a Mr Powell, who, being a friend of both parties was more than alarmed at this threat, for it was quite apparent that Hill meant what he said; but all he could do for the moment was to tell Hill that he would immediately warn Mountford of what was afoot.

Captain Hill recognised in Lord Mohun sitting opposite at

the table one who was as contentious and dashing, regardless of logic, as he was himself, so that when Charles voiced his support and offered himself as an ally (a mental picture already formed, no doubt, of his acting as a second to a nice duel) it did not really surprise the officer.

The two men agreed the abduction would take place the following night. A coach was ordered to be waiting for them at nine o'clock in Drury Lane, near the theatre, but only with two horses so as not to attract attention. Four more would be at readiness in the stables. Captain Hill would be calling for Mrs B. at the theatre on the first stage of abduction.

But things were not to turn out as planned, for Mrs Bracegirdle was not playing that night. The gallant abducters, disappointed, soon regained their spirits, for they learned she was supping at the house of Mr Page in Princes Street nearby, so that it was to there they repaired to watch this house that was just across the road from Lord Craven's.

When nine o'clock arrived with no movement, they began to think themselves misinformed and so ordered the coachman to drive to Howard Street, where Mrs B. lodged, in the house of a Mrs Browne.

Howard Street is a cross-way leading from Arundel Street, through Norfolk Street, to Surrey Street. Mr Mountford lived in Norfolk Street, so that it was not likely he could arrive home without a watcher spying him.

From their stationary coach Mohun and Hill became aware of a number of people seeming to gather loosely in front of the house of Mrs Bracegirdle.

This intrusion, possibly the result of a word of their intentions having been let slip by someone, caused them to alter plans, and they ordered the coachman to stand again in front of Mr Page's house.

They did not have to wait long. At ten o'clock his door opened and Mr Page came out escorting Mrs Bracegirdle, her mother and her brother. They soon noticed the coach, in front of Lord Craven's house, with the steps down. Looking in as they walked past, they were surprised to see Lord Mohun sitting in it with what appeared to be a number of pistols.

At this moment two soldiers, whom Captain Hill had organised, rushed forward, forced Mrs B. away from Mr Page and would have dragged her to the coach had not her mother clung to her, arms around her neck.

At this point, up rushed the gallant Captain who struck both Mr Page and the old lady with his sword. Some passers-by attempted to stop him and were successful enough to oblige him to withdraw his sword; but using his wits he contrived to persuade the onlookers that they were mistaken, he was, he said shielding the lady from danger and she required safe-conduct. He even persuaded Mrs Bracegirdle that he had no part in the fray, so she allowed him to escort her and her mother home. Lord Mohun and the soldiers followed as if in pursuit. Every now and then Hill swung round as though daring them to approach.

Upon reaching Howard Street Hill judged that it was now possible to carry out the original plan of forcible abduction, and the soldiers were dismissed.

Just as Captain Hill was about to leave the party outside Mrs Bracegirdle's door, he plucked Mr Page by the sleeve and let him know that he wanted to say something to him in private. Page, however, very keen to get back into his own house, replied hurriedly that 'another time would do; tomorrow would serve.'

It could be said with some justice that my Lord Mohun would have been better looking after his estate at Boconnoc rather than getting wilfully involved in the unworthy little drama that was developing. But he was enjoying it. He sensed action, the sound of clash of swords, and the thrill of events leading to the spilling of blood.

Mrs Bracegirdle and Mr Page managed to get safely into her house, quickly shutting the door behind them in the face of Captain Hill. This infuriated him and only made his resolution stronger to murder Mountford. With his accomplice Lord Mohun, he paced up and down the street for two hours waiting for Mountford to return home. Each had his sword drawn, a feature which greatly alarmed the little party in Mrs B's house.

Mrs Browne boldly went out to ask them what they were up to. The two conspirators were frank in their reply. They were awaiting the arrival of Mr Mountford.

It was clear that the besiegers had no intention of withdrawing for they obtained two bottles of wine and settled within easy reach of their quarry's house. The sight of the two, with drawn swords, drinking wine in the street late at night, attracted the attention of the Watch who inquired what they were doing with drawn swords in their hands?

At this moment two soldiers, whom Captain Hill had or- Peer of the realm, touch 'em if you dare!' a reply that was successful in flooring the Watch so that they went away, asking no more.

At midnight, the unfortunate Mr Mountford appeared at the end of the street, happily near home and bed, completely unaware of danger. Lord Mohun was the first to meet and speak to him, Mountford having expressed surprise at seeing him there at such an hour.

'I suppose you have been sent for?' asked Lord Mohun.

'No,' was his reply, puzzled, 'I'm on my way home from the Playhouse.' Lord Mohun went on, 'You know all about the lady, I imagine?' Mountford not understanding what he was getting at, replied, 'I hope that my wife has given you no offence?'

'You mistake me,' said Mohun, 'It is Mrs Bracegirdle I mean.'

'Mrs Bracegirdle is no concern of mine.' replied the actor. A pause followed. There was silence in the street, and only a dim oval outline showed where expression was hid.

Suddenly, Captain Hill started forward, 'There's no longer time for such discourse!' and saying it, he struck Mountford with his hand, followed instantly by a lunge, the sword being run through the victim's body.

Mountford did not immediately fall to the ground, and even began to draw his sword, but then he collapsed and sank onto the ground.

The mechanism of justice was set in motion, but here I need only refer to the improbable outcome. After a trial for murder that did not include Captain Hill, for he had escaped and vanished, Lord Mohun was cleared by his peers in the House of Lords, and was released, and this verdict was due to the gallant victim having affirmed, as he lay dying, that Lord Mohun had no share in the actual murder. Howls of protest were heard in coffee houses and read in newspapers complaining that the blood of the poor was shed with impunity by the great.

Perhaps because the Queen continued to keep him as colonel

of a regiment of Foot, thus retaining his self-confidence, he did not lose any of his fire and aggression, characteristics that burnt within this man of 'middle stature, inclining to fat, not thirty years old'.

At all events, a few years later he was involved in another murder. This was a similar venture which he shared with a man of higher stature than Captain Hill, the Earl of Warwick no less. He was once more pronounced innocent by the unanimous vote of the Peers.

This time, he pulled himself together, and before I move on to his final duel, I think it fair to substantiate this unlikely statement with a quote from a *History of Queen Anne*. It is against the date 11th March, 1713, London. Here it is:

> After this last misfortune, my Lord Mohun did wonderfully reclaim; and what by his reading, what by his conversation with the ablest statesmen, so well improved his natural parts that he became a great ornament to the peerage, and a strenuous asserter of the cause of Liberty, and the late Revolution, which last, however, could not raise him but many enemies, and is, I doubt, the only reason why his memory is so unfairly, so barbarously treated.
>
> It is true that my Lord Mohun, like most men in a cold climate, still lov'd a merry glass of wine with his friends .... He behaved himself so discreetly at the Court of Hanover whither he accompanied the late Earl of Macclesfield, whose niece he had married, that he left an excellent character behind him ...

The political situation which was behind the circumstances leading to Lord Mohun reverting to his old ways and challenging the Duke of Hamilton are too tedious to relate here, but the circumstance of the insult are these.

On Thursday, 15th November 1711, a party was assembled at the chambers of Mr Orlebar, a master in Chancery, when the Duke of Hamilton made some reflections on Mr Whitworth, father of the Queen's late ambassador to the Czar.

At this Lord Mohun furiously exclaimed that the Duke had neither truth nor justice in him. The Duke of Hamilton made no reply, and both parties remained at the table for half an hour after this outbreak.

On parting, the Duke of Hamilton made a low bow to Mohun, who returned the civility, and these gracious salutations led the onlookers to believe that that would be the end of the clash.

But Lord Mohun had no such idea. He was determined to take this opportunity to fight this political and personal enemy, even so far as to break the rules to gain this end. Mohun was the one who gave offence, yet next day it was he who sent a challenge to the Duke by the hand of General Macartney, a friend.

In the evening the Duke, accompanied by Colonel John Hamilton, went to meet the General at a tavern. The Duke and General Macartney were in one room while Mohun and Colonel Hamilton were in one adjoining. Between these four, the time and the place of the duel were agreed upon.

On the Sunday morning, 15th November, at seven o'clock, Lord Mohun with his second, the General, drove in a hackney-coach to the Lodge of Hyde Park where they alighted. Soon after they were met by the Duke of Hamilton and his second. They jumped over a ditch into a place called the Nursery.

Lord Mohun wished to dispense with the seconds, but the Duke insisted they should bear their part in the engagement as 'Mr Macartney should have a share in the dance.'

It has been said that the Duke, most reasonably one would think, was from the very first unwilling to fight, and even at the last moment would have consented to a reconciliation. At the inquiry that took place on the 26th, Colonel Hamilton in his evidence stated that, before he was half dressed, the Duke called at his house and hurried him into his chariot 'so soon that he had to finish the buttoning of his waistcoat there'.

By the time they got into Pall Mall the Duke observed that the Colonel had left his sword behind, whereupon he stopped the chariot and gave the footman a bunch of keys and orders to fetch a mourning sword out of the relevant closet. On the return of the footman they drove on to Hyde Park where the coachman stopped. The Duke then ordered him to drive on to Kensington.

When they approached the Lodge they saw a hackney-coach at a distance, at which the Duke said there was somebody he must speak with; but driving up to it and seeing nobody he asked the coachman, where were the gentlemen he had brought? He indicated a little way ahead. The Duke and the Colonel got out and walked over a rise toward the pond where they came upon Lord Mohun and General Macartney.

As soon as the Duke came within hearing of them he said that he hoped he was come in time, and Macartney answered, 'In very good time, my Lord.'

In reply, the Duke said, 'Sir, you are the cause of this! Let the event be what it will. Macartney replied, 'We'll have our share.' Then the Duke said, 'There is my friend then; he will take his share in my dance!'

The Duke then looked about, above and around him. Then he said quietly, 'How grey and cold London looks this morning, and yet the sky is almost cloudless.'

'It is through lack of London smoke,' said Macartney, 'London is nothing without its smoke.'

The combat between the principles then commenced, and at a little distance from them, between the seconds.

The clash of steel drew the attention of the Park Keepers and a few stragglers who were abroad at this early hour. None of them interfered. They looked on as they might a cock-fight.

In a short time Mohun had wounded the Duke in both legs, and in the groin, and then the arm and other parts of the body. Each at the same time managed to make a desperate lunge at the other, each dropping inadvertently his defence. The effect was dramatic because the Duke was somehow able to thrust his sword through Mohun's stomach right up to the hilt. This did not prevent Lord Mohun summoning up enough strength to 'shorten' his sword and plunging it into the upper part of the Duke's breast, the blade running downwards into his belly, Lord Mohun then fell to the ground.

The Park Keepers and others to the number of nine or ten then came up, and the Duke was found to have a wound on the left side which came in between the left shoulder and pap, and went slanting down through the midriff into his belly.

Some thought it impracticable for Lord Mohun to have given him such a wound, and a belief was current that General Macartney had been evil enough to do it. At all events, the General fled to Holland to escape any consequences.

An attempt was made to remove the Duke to what was described as the Cake House, but it was not to be. The duel was over, and without a victor, for both the Duke and Lord Mohun died from their wounds.

Later in the day, in a dramatic report in a letter to Mrs Dingley, Jonathan Swift related the story as he learnt it:

> This morning at eight, my man brought me word that the Duke of Hamilton had fought with Lord Mohun and killed him, and was brought home wounded. I immediately sent him to the Duke's house in St James's Square, but the porter could hardly answer him for tears, and a great rabble was about the house. They fought at seven this morning.
>
> The dog Mohun was killed on the spot; but while the Duke was over him, Mohun, shortening his sword, stabbed him in at the shoulder to the heart.
>
> The Duke was helped towards the Cake House by the Ring in Hyde Park, and died on the grass before he could reach it: and was brought home in his coach by eight while the poor Duchess was asleep. Mohun gave the affront and yet sent the challenge.
>
> I am infinitely concerned for the poor Duke who was a frank, honest, good-natured man. I loved him very well, and I think he loved me better.

The reader will note that Swift takes the ritual of duelling entirely for granted, registering no comment about its savagery. This puzzled me. Duels seemed to occur frequently, yet no protests are heard across the centuries about what appears to us as a display of immature, rather obscene, barbarity. There was obviously something much more than this to it which merited Society's acquiescence, so I set about the task of tracing contemporary views.

We shall shortly be looking at another duel in which the current Lord of Boconnoc indulged. But before considering it let me give the views on duelling at the period at which this duel of Lord Camelford's took place, namely, the end of the eighteenth century.

Here is the sage of the age speaking, giving most revealing reflections on the ethics of the custom; and this coming from a scholar rather than a man of action, surely makes these conclusions most surprising.

This is Boswell relating Johnson's dicta:

> The subject of duelling was introduced. 'There is no case in England,' said the Doctor, 'where one or other of the combatants *must* die; if you have overcome your adversary by disarming him, that is sufficient, though you should not kill him; your honour, or the honour of your family, is restored as much as it can be by a duel. It is cowardly to force your antagonist to renew the combat, when you know that you have the advantage. You might just as well go and cut his throat while he is asleep in bed.
>
> 'When a duel begins, it is supposed there may be an equality because it is not always skill that prevails. It depends much on presence of mind, nay, on accidents. The wind may be in a man's face. He may fall. Many such things may decide superiority.
>
> 'A man is sufficiently punished by being called out and subject to the risk that is in a duel.' But on my suggesting that the injured person is equally subjected to risk, he fairly owned he could not explain the rationality of duelling.'

On another occasion Boswell asked to have settled whether it was contrary to the laws of Christianity, or, at least, morality. This was at a dinner at General Oglethorpe's at which Johnson and Oliver Goldsmith were also present. Answering the question the 'brave old General fired at this and said, with a lofty air, "Undoubtedly a man has a right to defend his honour".'

Oliver Goldsmith then turned to Boswell and asked him what he would do 'if he were affronted'. Boswell replied that he would think it necessary to fight. 'Why then,' said Goldsmith, 'that solves the question,' at which the following dialogue took place:

'No, sir,' said Johnson, 'it doesn't solve the question. It does not follow that what a man would do is therefore right.' Boswell persisted in his request, 'was duelling contrary to the laws of Christianity?'

> Johnson [writes Boswell] immediately entered on the subject and treated it in a masterly manner. . . . . . 'Sir,' he said, 'as men become in a high degree refined, various causes of

offence arise which are considered to be of such importance that life must be staked to atone for them, though in reality they are not so.

'A body that has received a very fine polish may be easily hurt. Before men arrive at this artificial refinement, if one tells his neighbour he lies, his neighbour tells him he lies; if one gives his neighbour a blow his neighbour gives him a blow.

'But in a state of highly polished society, an affront is held to be a serious injury. It must therefore be resented, or rather a duel must be fought upon it; as men have agreed to banish from their society one who puts up with an affront without fighting a duel.

'Now, Sir, it is never unlawful to fight in self-defence. He, then, who fights a duel, does not fight from passion against his antagonist, but out of self-defence; to avert the stigma of the world and to prevent himself being driven out of society. I could wish there was not that superfluity of refinement; but while such notions prevail, no doubt a man may lawfully fight a duel.'

While on this subject, Horace Walpole later wrote his view of duelling at this time (1773) in *Journal of the Reign of George III*. He wrote, 'The age of duelling had of late much revived ...... and many attempts were made in print and on the stage to curb so horrid and absurd a practice.'

In 1718 Lord Mohun's widow sold Boconnoc, and all her other property to Thomas Pitt, whose grandson was the great William Pitt, Earl of Chatham, Prime Minister of England during much of the Napoleonic War. There is an interesting record of this transaction. This Thomas Pitt was at the time well known throughout Europe as the Governor of Fort St George in Madras, and it was while he was there that he bought the celebrated jewel known as the Pitt diamond.

He had purchased this stone in 1701 from one of the eminent diamond merchants, Jamehund, for £20,000. The cutting of it cost £5,000, and the chips and filings were valued at £7,000.

Thomas Pitt let it be known to Queen Anne that it was for sale but she claimed no interest in it, and it was later sold to the Duke of Orleans, the Regent of France during the minority of

Louis XV. The price paid was £135,000, £5,000 being spent apparently in negotiating the deal. The weight of the diamond was 136½ carats, its value as estimated by a commission of jewellers in 1791 was twelve million livres.

The Kings of France wore this faultless brilliant in their hats, so Lake and other historians assert; and Napoleon Buonaparte had it set in the mouth of a crocodile which formed the pommel of his sword. It will be of interest to some for me to mention that it was found in Malacca in a famous mine of Porteal, and was a somewhat round stone, one inch broad, one and one-sixth of an inch long, and three-fourths of an inch thick.

Thanks to this little pile, Thomas Pitt was able to buy Boconnoc, with half the sum to spare, and then settled there to live. One of the first things he did was to add another wing to the house. On his death he was succeeded by one of his two sons, Thomas. This Thomas was created Baron Camelford in 1784 when his first cousin became Prime Minister at the age of twenty-five, filling this high office for almost half his life span of forty-six years.

There appears now on the scene the second Lord Camelford who was born in 1775. Born Thomas Pitt, the baby started life the centre of a grand celebration at Boconnoc where a large concourse was gathered for the festivities, and where the feature, second only to the infant's presence, was a major wrestling competition with silver trophies as prizes.

Henceforth, the boyhood of Thomas was to be denied the pleasures of company, his parents spending long periods away, both abroad and in London at Camelford House, and elsewhere. Thomas was left largely to grow up with the steward of the Estate as guide, and a resident tutor for his education. Companionship of his own age was denied him, even his sister Annette, three years older than he and of whom he was very fond, was rarely left at Boconnoc but accompanied their parents on their long visits far afield. Years later Annette came to marry Lord Grenville, a man who held high political office and suffered much embarrassment through Thomas's misdeeds.

This isolation was to have its effect on Thomas later, for his bursting energies were entrapped by the bonds of his enclosed and lonely life. Boconnoc, much as he liked its variety, its grandeur that rested so easily in the parkland setting, its strange, brooding power from the silent presence of large empty rooms, and its echoing cellars, all these appealed to his adventurous instincts, but they were not people, not children of his own age.

As he grew older, frustration turned to resentment and showed itself in a way that was to remain with him, a disdain for authority, a rejection of the attitude assumed by adults that they know best.

His father came to realise this and, like many a parent before and after, thought the way to check this feature of his character was to send him to boarding school. Accordingly, at the age of eleven he was taken by his parents to a school in Switzerland, to Neuchatel where, after a doubtful start he settled down to make the best of once more being left alone by his parents. I say 'make the best of it', for it seems this really was so, and that, in spite of the feeling of rejection he had to live with, he nevertheless found he owed much to this sojourn of some three years in Switzerland; for in his Will he directed that he should be buried beneath a certain tree on an island in the Lac du Bienne, and this request was, in due course, carried out.

In 1789, Lord Camelford brought his son back to England for his further education, and in July he started his scholastic studies at the still famous school, Charterhouse. This was Thomas's first experience of communal life, with its disciplines and rules in favour of the many for the ultimate good of the individual.

In Neuchatel the atmosphere had been one of a large family, something very far removed from the forbidding rigours of an English boarding school; something very different, too, from the respectful persuasions to which the Steward of Boconnoc had necessarily to limit himself when being responsible for the heir to the great manor and estate of the Camelfords.

Physical bullying at Charterhouse was rife, and it was not to Tom's liking. After only a few days he ran away, not taking, unfortunately, any lesson from it with him, unless it was the conviction of the efficacy of brute force in argument instead of words, a belief he pursued throughout his life to the discomfort of his victims.

However, it is fair to say that, unlike the usual bully, he

became a man of dash and courage and colour as well, an ornament to any scene but like a storm cloud, more beautiful from a distance than near to.

When he was six years old, Tom had been taken to Plymouth to have a look at the Fleet that was assembling in the Sound. This was a magnificent sight for the boy, and was almost certainly, I have judged, the Grand Fleet sent, under Lord Howe, to relieve Gibraltar. The French had recently recaptured Minorca for the second time, and were now no doubt preparing to reduce Gibraltar.

The Navy had already twice replenished the garrison's stores, but its endurance could not last indefinitely, and so it was resolved to send out the Fleet referred to above to effect the Rock's relief.

Little wonder it fired Tom Pitt's imagination for it must have been a wonderful sight on the blue waters of Plymouth Sound. Lord Howe hoisted his flag in the Victory: and around this remarkable vessel gathered a wonderful assemblage of transports, storeships and mechantmen, numbering in all no less than 183 sail.

These were preparations of an unprecedented scale and made an abiding impression on the boy's mind, so genuinely it seems, that his father condoned with his running away from Charterhouse and arranged for him to join the Navy. On 25th September 1787, he enrolled as 'Captain's Servant' on board HMS *Tobago*.

This, however, was only a procedural appointment of a technical nature, and it was not until the required period had passed in which to qualify for a commission that he finally joined a ship. This was a sloop, the *Guardian*, and he joined her at Spithead on 9th September 1789.

This was a good moment for anyone to join the Navy, for the result of the War of American Independence, with the shame, surrender and disillusion of defeat that it left with our armed forces, had had one good result of huge importance for the nation. Not only did defeat act as a stimulus to the high command, but as a tonic to the administration on which the Fleet depended for sustenance.

Callender, in *The Naval Side of British History* tells of the state of inefficiency the Fleet had been allowed to drift from a lofty complacency that had bemused the politicians. But now the dockyards and victualling yards were overhauled, and to all practical purposes refashioned and rebuilt. The walls were repaired and heightened, and trustworthy guards placed at every gate.

Stocktaking was instituted, inspections made frequent and systematic. The rope-walks, sail-lofts, anchor-walks and bake-houses were made secure against theft and embezzlement, and stores were controlled by the issue of checks and counterfoils.

It is of this period that Callender brings in an interesting commentary on our Tom's cousin William Pitt, the young Premier. I quote:

> In a material sense the Navy began to prosper, as it had not done since the days of the Commonwealth, and the equipping of a battlefleet ceased to be a labour of Hercules and became a simple matter of routine.
>
> There is a widespread belief that this welcome consummation should be attributed to the personal agency of William Pitt. But for such a belief there would appear to be little or no foundation.
>
> Like so many of his countrymen, the young Premier of 1784 did not understand or appreciate the sea service, or not until the cataclysm in France awakened his interest.
>
> Most of the present [1920] dockyard buildings seem to have been completed in the year in which he first assumed office, and therefore must have been sanctioned while the American war was still in progress, and while money for the fighting services was granted without question. In 1778, the year in which the French took up arms against us, the naval votes amounted to £875,000; in the year in which Pitt came into power they had risen to upwards of two millions.
>
> It was, perhaps, inevitable that the apostle of economy should at the close of a war insist upon naval reductions; but if he cannot be credited with the maritime sense of the Tudor kings, he did not incur the reproach attaching to his predecessors . . . .
>
> When, therefore, the French Revolution broke out . . . the Royal Navy was, in a material sense, as sound and wholesome as the emergency demanded. The ships were ready to

take to sea at a moment's notice; and the [dock] yards roomier and more accommodating than they had ever been before, were prepared to cope expeditiously with any reasonable requirements. ...

I am going to interpolate here a reference to something that does not really concern us, and nor did it concern personally Tom Pitt. I am going to do this for two reasons: first, the loss of a great ship, the *Royal George* in Portsmouth, occurred about the same time that Tom saw the majestic sight of the Fleet in Plymouth Sound that inspired him later to join the Navy; and secondly because the recovery from the bottom of the Solent of this great ship is far advanced and will be of major national interest when finally put on view.

The *Royal George*, which had carried Hawke into battle at Quiberon Bay, was being heeled over so that her underwater timbers could receive attention. The angle of inclination was not great, and in no way worried the nine hundred souls then onboard.

Admiral Kempenfelt was at work in his cabin, pen in hand, doubtless looking forward to the fleet effecting the salvation of Gibraltar.

Suddenly, a sickening crack or giant rent startled everyone. It was as if the hull had been crushed by a vast weight. Orders were instantly given to right the ship. The order was carried out. There was no panic.

However, the unbelievable happened. The great vessel began to settle and then suddenly sank. An eye-witness said that it sank like a leaden coffin into the deep. The Admiral and nearly all those on board lost their lives. This terrible spectacle was seen by watching thousands on shore and in ships who could do nothing to help, so quickly did it all happen.

Callender continues: 'The tragedy sent a thrill of horror throughout the land, and before very long Cowper's solemn monody "Toll for the Brave", was tugging at men's heart strings and inducing all the charitable to contribute generously for the widows and children.'

The subsequent court-martial examined all the survivors. It was unanimously agreed that the vessel had been so long neglected that decay had eaten deep into her vitals and that the underpart of the *Royal George* had literally dropped from under her. It is here that Callender makes his historical assessment.

'In a word,' he writes, 'Kempenfelt and his gallant fellows were the victims of the corrupt administration which had lately also forfeited North America.'

Now, to return to Tom Pitt and his first ship, the *Guardian*. As she sailed down the Channel, Tom's emotions were those of any young man's first appointment to a ship in the Navy: a feeling of disbelief and excitement that at last he had grown up, had left the no man's land of the teens and was now, with men as colleagues accepting him, employed to do a man's job. Little did Tom realise the hazards that awaited him on the voyage, and the times he would be dreaming nostalgically of the tall trees and the rolling parkland that encircled Boconnoc, and wishing he were back there. Midshipman Pitt was fourteen years old, and he was taking the first step toward a stormy naval career in which his ambitious, intolerant, arrogant character was far more often to be the creator of the storms than were the elements.

The *Guardian*, Captain Riou, was bound for Australia, to the recently settled colony at Port Jackson, New South Wales. On board was a cargo of supplies for the settlement, which consisted at this stage of mainly convicts transported in an expedition that had been despatched only the year before the *Guardian's* voyage. This first expedition had, incidentally, as its second-in command, a Cornishman, Lieutenant Philip G. King, born at Launceston, and they first landed at Botany Bay before moving south to Port Jackson.

The *Guardian* now had onboard another group of male and female convicts, as well as ordinary, though venturesome, passengers. They called in at Santa Cruz, in the Canary Islands, to take on two thousand gallons of wine to add to the cargo and then, after a stay of a few days, upped anchor and set course for the Cape which they reached on 24th November. Here supplies were replenished and others taken onboard as cargo, and the ship was headed across the Southern Pacific for Australia. A solitary voyage lay before them, some six thousand miles of empty ocean, empty excepting in the southern regions through which lay their course, where huge icebergs silently lurked in fog and darkness.

And it was one of these that brought disaster. The *Guardian* was going well, cleaving her way through the waters, and taking full advantage of the cold westerly trade wind filling her sails from astern. On this day in question a fog began to form in the afternoon and visibility was gradually reduced. This did not worry Captain Riou so much because he was sailing his ship through a vast ocean on which he did not expect to meet another vessel during the whole of two months.

Then, very suddenly and with no warning, the curtain of fog drew apart, and to his horror, and far too late to avoid, he saw a huge white rugged cliff face straight ahead, with the top of it, high up above the masts, disappearing into the mist.

Into this the *Guardian* crashed and immediately began to take in water, but soon it was realised that by some miracle the hull was not badly damaged. A horrifying possibility was soon apparent, for there was a high cleft in the iceberg, like a tall cavern but without its roof, and it was into this trap that it seemed the ship must have been driven. Captain Riou ordered boats to be lowered, knowing full well there were not enough places to take more than half a crew. It was now nearly dark and, mercifully, the sea was moderate, but the movement of the ship hitting and scraping, made an awesome cavalcade of noise. Onboard, this was soon added to by the drunken shouts of those men who had broken into the liquor store and were hopelessly drunk.

Everything, including the guns, was now thrown over-board to lighten ship, while two manned boats were got away, only one of which survived. It was the launch and it was spotted by a French merchant vessel on her way to the Cape, the *Guardian's* last port of call. Among those left on board was young Tom Pitt, who, when news from the Cape got through to England of the disaster four months later, was assumed dead.

But somehow, Captain Riou and his vessel survived the night and next morning managed to extricate themselves from the iceberg's cold embrace. Though the pumps had to be manned all the time, the *Guardian* bravely surmounted what had seemed a fatal situation, and slowly lumbered back through freezing seas westward along the track she had recently come, until she arrived at Table Bay two months later.

Tom Pitt waited at the Cape for passage home, and before

long he joined the homeward bound packet *Prince of Orange* which berthed at Harwich in September 1790. His frightening experience on his first voyage did nothing to make Tom draw back from his desire to serve in the Navy. What is strange is that although no detail is known of his life on the *Guardian*, it is known that at a future date when, fiercely ambitious, he was most anxious to be promoted lieutenant and needed references from those whom he had served under, Captain Riou replied to the official request for his views by saying Mr Pitt had unfortunately conducted himself on occasions in such a manner that his (Captain Riou's) experience of these failures precluded him from supporting the promotion.

Indeed, from now on Tom Pitt's impetuous nature was further exacerbated by not getting his own way at all times, and this became a fixation that the world was unjustly against him, particularly the Navy who showed natural reluctance to give him as swift a process of promotion as he deemed himself worthy of. This merely increased his aggression, fed now on an absolute conviction that his advancement was being deliberately and unfairly witheld.

It is not surprising, therefore, that once his father had died, and he became Lord Camelford of Boconnoc, his antagonism to any restrictions he believed deliberately imposed upon him led to a series of incidents and scandals that could really only end in the pressure of violence imposed by him on others being found a target, out of control, and vented on himself.

The stepping stones that led to his death in a totally unnecessary duel, which he furiously pressed upon his innocent opponent, were often bizarre, generally trivial in their origin, and always unkind on others.

And yet, the infuriating thing about him which kept him friends under the most provocative conditions, was that there was a heart beating under his martial tunic, a heart that incongruously retained a sense of romance, even sentimentality, even contrition. These gentle emotions fit the nature of all bullies, and the second Lord Camelford, splendid to look at, tall, well-built and full of spirit, certainly bore the ingredients for such an opinion. He had, however, a saving grace that even his enemies admitted to. He was a brave man, and a man who, if he had more self-control might well have helped make history in the Navy.

Shortly after his return from the dramatic disaster of his first assignment in the Navy, Tom Pitt was more eager than ever to take another post afloat. Accordingly, thanks to his influential relations, he was appointed a midshipman aboard the *Discovery* (Captain Vancouver), a vessel being prepared to leave on an important expedition to chart the north-west coast of America, a task that would involve all on board being three years away from home. Going with the *Discovery*, as escort, was one other ship, the *Chatham*.

Captain George Vancouver had great experience of such a mission, having served on each of Cook's voyages of exploration. This time he was in command of a sloop, broadly following Cook's track to the North Pacific, but then going on to new uncharted territory. Vancouver Island was named so at this time.

Such a voyage must inevitably attract serious unrest from time to time among a crew of a hundred of so men living on top of one another in conditions of sometimes extreme discomfort and with deprivation of all ordinary off-duty distractions and varied diet. Tom was fortunate in one respect: he found a good friend among the midshipmen who understood his hot-headed temperament, and who remained a good friend till Tom's death.

There was a time, for example, of extreme tension when the *Discovery* anchored off Tahiti. Cook had been here and his crew had brought back wonderful reports of the beautiful maidens and their delicious attractions made smilingly and immediately available to the visitors.

One can imagine, therefore, that the discomforts and dangers of the long voyage from England, round the Cape and then across the Pacific, was often made bearable by the fantasies evoked by the prospect of this jewel of delight.

Captain Vancouver had had experience of the cost of this fraternisation and the unrest it caused; and the legacy of disease it left behind in the Islands. Captain Bligh who had arrived back in England shortly before the *Discovery* had sailed, had also warned of his experiences and the outcome of free intercourse with the natives. The quarrels and unrest that accompanied this were a contributory factor to the unrest that led to the mutiny on the *Bounty*.

Captain Vancouver gave his orders, that no one was to be allowed ashore and no contact with the natives of any sort would be allowed. There was, of course, resentment and grumbling, but acceptance because of the scale and type of punishment that was inflicted in the event of disobeyment of orders.

It was left to Thomas Pitt to chance his hand at softening the crash of the lost expectations; and unfortunately for him, the Captain was watching.

It was strictly forbidden to barter anything with ship's equipment, a reasonable restriction, quite apart from the fact it implied an element of fraternisation. Tom was on deck watching the canoes bobbing about in the ruffled water around the ship when he spotted a girl with lithesome figure and come-hither eyes who was too pretty to allow to go by unheeded, especially as she subtly made her interest in him apparent.

The most valuable thing to barter with was iron, so when Captain Vancouver saw this midshipman go below, then come up again with an iron hoop from a barrel and pass it down to the girl, there was no stopping the march of discipline, and Tom was flogged for his moment of empty romance.

The strain imposed on the crew of the *Discovery* by their enclosed proximity also imposed an almost impossible task on the captain. Strict, even severe, discipline just had to be maintained, but restrictions of this nature could be the better borne if harsh discipline was linked by a captain to humane leadership. The crew might find it hard to love him, but they could respect him. So far as Captain Vancouver was concerned, though he failed to be able to earn the respect of Tom Pitt, one of his fourteen young, spirited midshipmen, the success of this marathon three-year voyage, spent in outlandish areas from California to Alaska, in extremes of weather, and with no shore company, is convincing evidence of Vancouver's worth as a leader. As for Tom's opinion, his contemptuous attitudes could pardonably have invoked in the captain on many occasions an understandable desire to murder the young gentleman.

Such an occasion I can imagine was when Tom, by some playful, irresponsible manner, contrived to break the glass of the compass binnacle while ragging about with another midshipman. The compass is the nerve centre of a ship, and a replacement glass fitting is not something you can find in the

North Pacific, and unlikely to be amongst ship's stores, so that it was a clear example of reckless behaviour, of a nature that Vancouver judged as meriting another flogging. This obviously did not do anything toward a better understanding between captain and midshipman. Nor did an occasion when Tom was found asleep on duty.

Captain Vancouver seized an unexpected opportunity to get rid of this stormy petrel. While the *Discovery* was at Hawaii fitting out for a return visit to the American coast, a British supply ship called and before she sailed on her return voyage Midshipman Pitt was placed on board.

The ship sailed in February, 1794, and her course was easterly. Arrived in Australia Tom heard the news that, his father having died a year before, he was now Lord Camelford of Boconnoc.

To do Tom justice the news did no more to him than redouble his ambition to make a name on his own account, and so, in spite of his recent unhappy experience in the *Discovery*, he decided to stay in the Navy, and where better for opportunities to distinguish himself than in a war theatre?

The outcome of this was that, he eventually found himself on a merchant ship sailing to India which put into the Dutch port of Malacca; and there lying in the roads was a British frigate, the *Resistance*, of 44 guns. Captain Packenham accepted him, and from the first, Tom was delighted to find that things were going to be much better. Captain Packenham liked him, and drew the best out of him. Incredibly, and to his disbelief and joy, Tom was promoted, within three weeks, to acting lieutenant. He was to serve on the *Resistance* for nearly a year.

In due course the captain wrote to the Admiralty in January, 1795 informing them that Camelford was a very promising young officer.

Regrettably, as soon as Tom got back to England, he became at odds with everything and everyone again, resuming his spectacular progress of bucolic invective and disdain for other people.

Here follows a list of some of the extraordinary episodes his fiery spirit provoked, his antagonism to all and sundry, but carried through with a panache, a warped enthusiasm with which, though he acted in the grand style, was never free of the bully's lust to impose humiliation.

I have no space to detail these somewhat sordid events; for my loyalty is to Boconnoc and the fact that within comparatively few years, compared to its age, it sired two babies each of whom grew with a weapon of violence at the ready, yet fell to violence, and in a circumstance created by himself.

This is not to say that, viewed from this distance, the story is not fascinating against a social background of an era of cultural and national virility. To the reader who would like to read more on this, let me have the privilege of referring him to a splendid book, fairly recently published and written by the historian Nikolai Tolstoy. *The Half-Mad Lord* is superbly researched and delightfully written from contemporary sources denied other less scholarly writers.

Here is a list of some of the scenes that led to the final drop of the curtain:
  Captain Vancouver challenged to duel
  Attempt to pressgang Barbados natives
  Shoots Lieutenant Peterson dead at point blank range
  Provokes, and shares in, Bond Street mob fight
  Spying trip to France — Cloak and dagger
  Violent scene at the 'Circus'
  Violent scene at Drury Lane.

So it went on, a dreary catalogue of exhibitionism making a nuisance of himself, invoking violence on the defenceless.

We now approach the end, but before doing so, it is only fair to say that the Reverend W. Cockburne, who was Tom's cousin, said of him that the world would perhaps have difficulty in believing it, but that Christianity was the constant subject of his reflections, his reading and his conversation.

And so to the last Act.

In 1804, the war against Napoleon was developing into one with menacing possibilities. There was a lively invasion scare; while Nelson was blockading Toulon over a period of weeks and months; and the Battle of Trafalgar was on the horizon. England depended almost wholly at this time on its Navy.

But at this moment of national danger Lord Camelford was nowhere near his erstwhile gallant shipmates. For him, his martial prowess was directed to such important events as an angry display in a coffee shop in Conduit Street, when a customer took one of two candles from his lordship's table. A fight was avoided when the young offender, a dandy, took flight when the waiter told him whom he was up against.

However, Lord Camelford was soon to be granted the opportunity to have all the excitement he craved and more than he cared for.

One of his friends was a young, good-looking Army officer called Best. He was not of the peerage but nevertheless a smart, entertaining young man who was admired for being one of the best pistol shots in the country, not least by Camelford.

One of his wide range of pleasurable interests in London that the dignified aspect of Boconnoc could not compete with was the company of lovely ladies of fortune such as, for example, petite, mischievous, and appropriately consoling Mrs Simmons who was currently being 'kept' by his lordship.

Mrs Simmons was friendly, too, with Mr Best, though we do not know if his liaison had terminated in the sense of pleasures sensual. It is apparent, however, that they were still seeing one another because a mutual friend told Camelford that Best had spoken slightingly of him to Mrs Simmons, a happening that some would have taken only as gossip not worth a moment's thought; but to Camelford's fiery temper the remark was the signal to play his part as the courageous, outraged gentleman, with its permitted exciting sequel, the avenging of his honour in the only way he could gain satisfaction.

It was, however, a day or so later that he made his challenge. It was on 6th March 1804 that, sitting at a table in the Prince of Wales's Coffee House in Oxford Street, he saw Best come in. Jumping noisily out of his chair he said to Best, in a loud voice for all to hear, that he had been told that Best had spoken of him in most 'unwarrantable' terms.

Rather taken aback, Best, remaining calm, replied he had no idea to what he was referring. Lord Camelford then in a loud voice, and furious, showered Best with invective as he repeated what he had heard Best had said to Mrs Simmons, finishing by calling him a scoundrel, a liar and a ruffian!

There was only one sequel to such an insult being made publicly, and Best did exactly what Lord Camelford had designed. He sent him a challenge, but with it an assurance that his lordship had been misinformed as no such words had ever passed his lips.

Camelford would not listen to this, and so a meeting was arranged for the following morning in Kensington.

It is possible that the reason for this, and similar irrational actions, could be traced to Camelford's pride being very badly wounded on the occasion of his leaving the Navy five years before in 1799. The contrived challenge was clearly exploited, for Camelford was to write a note absolving Best from all blame. Probably it could be largely attributed to his sense of failure, the ignominy he had suffered earlier resulting from his resigning from the Navy just when a fine career of action was opening up for him.

The reason for this drastic decision to leave the Navy stemmed from his undertaking a ridiculous and dangerous task which he adjudged would gain him a lasting place in the gallery of heroes.

On 18th January 1804 he set off by coach to Dover, heavily disguised with nondescript clothes and close-cropped hair. With him he carried two pistols, ball, powder and a stubby two-edged dagger. Arrived at Dover he attracted unwanted attention by seeking a fisherman who would take him to France and land him on a beach near Calais. As a law had recently been passed forbidding anyone either entering England from France, or leaving England for France, it was not surprising the locals were interested and the self-appointed white knight was seized in the boat just after it had pushed off from the shore.

His Lordship, whose spectacular plan was to murder one or more of the Directory in Paris, was bundled into a coach in which he was taken under escort back to London to face the shame of ridicule.

However, his ignominy was framed in gracious circumstances to start with, for the whole of the Privy Council was called to examine the matter. Among the PC's was none other than his brother-in-law, the luckless Lord Grenville who was able to by-pass the embarrassment of sharing in the investigation by being unavoidably absent.

The outcome of the enquiry was that Lord Camelford, who was still, it must be remembered, in the Navy, was adjudged unsuitable to hold command in future, of any ship in the King's service. Such an edict was something impossible to bear, and the shattered Camelford tendered his resignation which was accepted.

50 The Living Breath of Cornwall

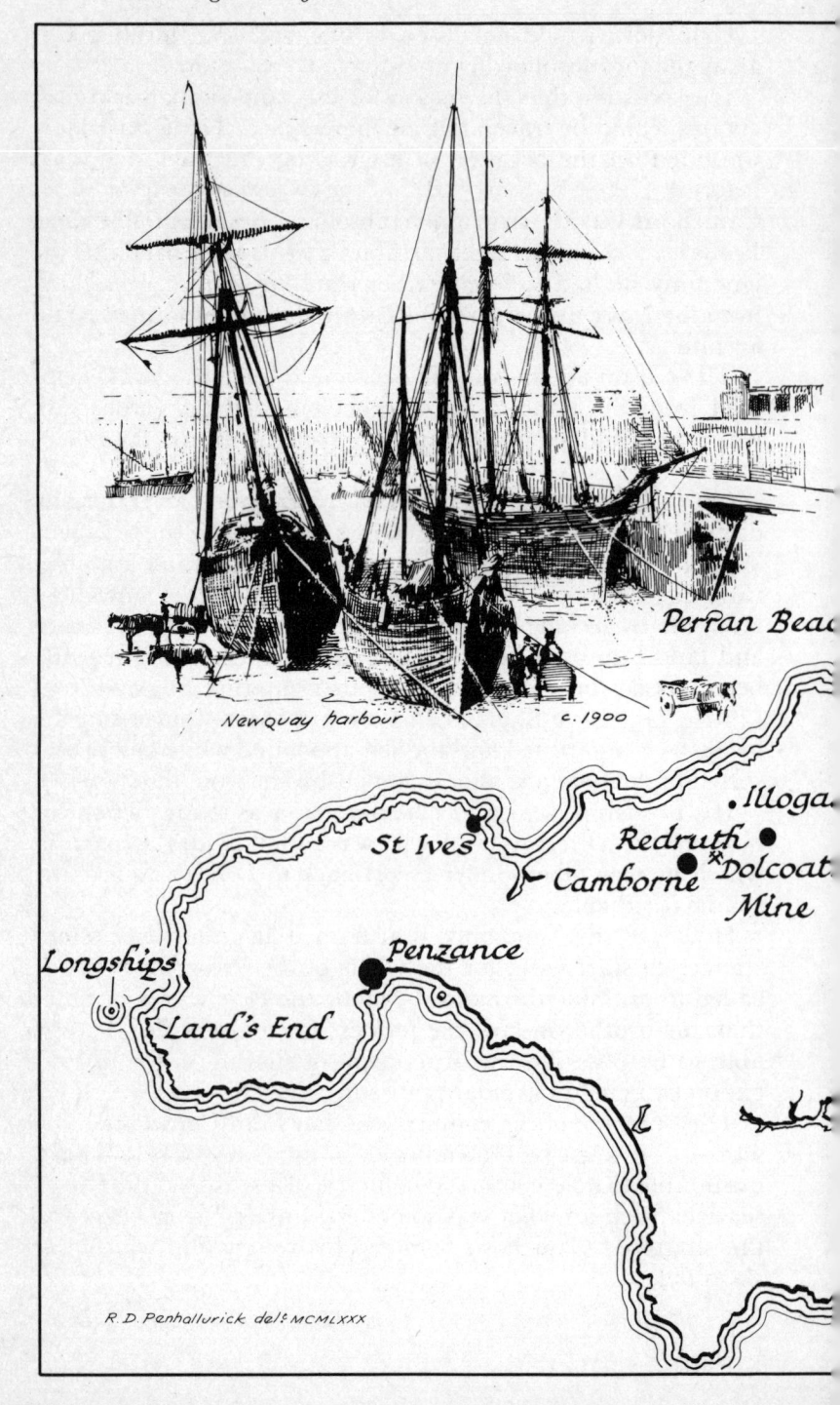

My Lord Impetuous, of Boconnoc 51

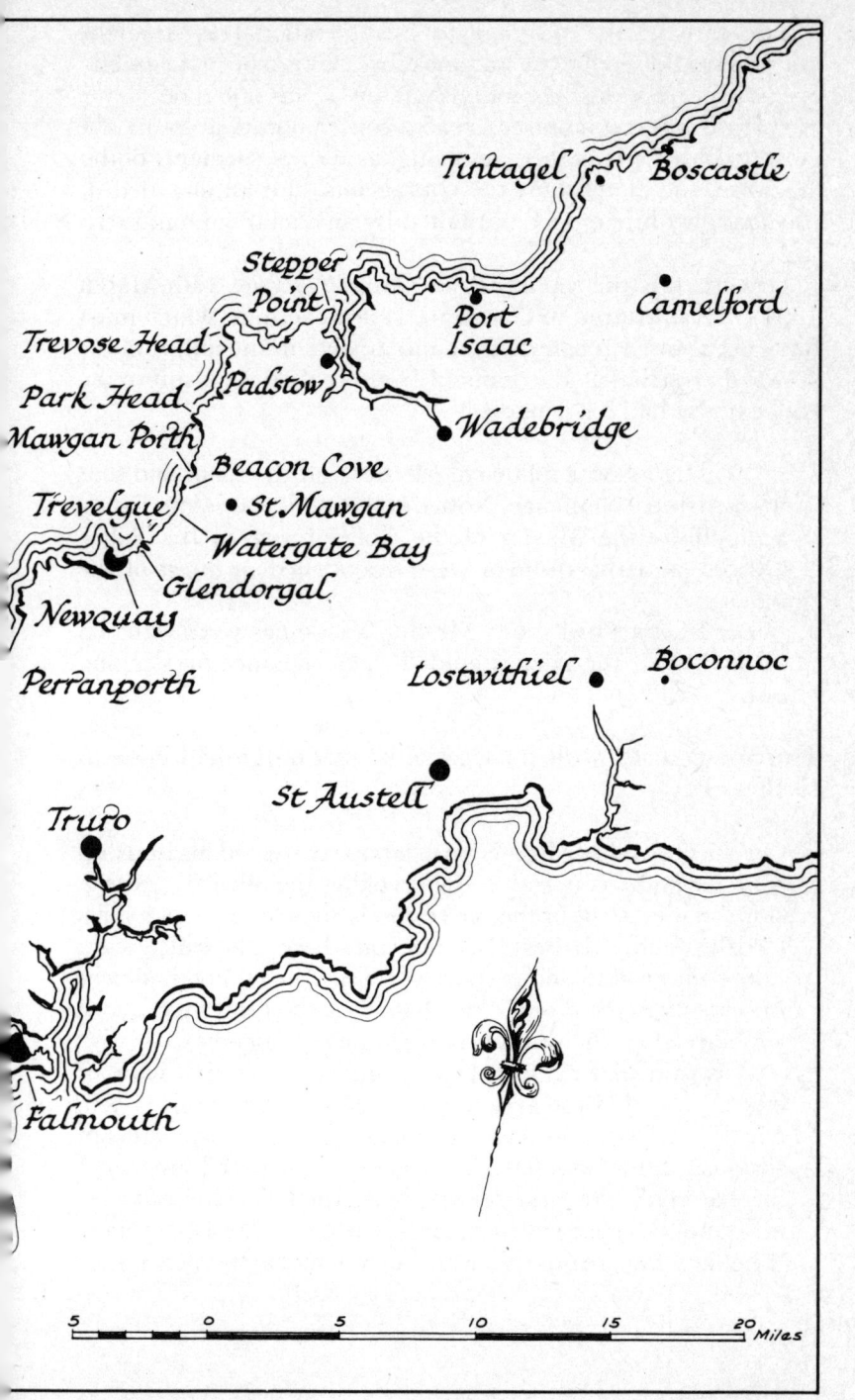

The provocation he gave to Best, irrational as it might appear, would seem to be but one more effort to be in the public eye as a fearless, dashing individual; but it was not to be.

It lends interest if one can read a contemporary account of a period affair such as this, involving, as it does, elements of the macabre, the glamorous, the courageous, and all included in the shadowy lure of vice promoted by any act of human sacrifice.

Here then is the report (*Royal Cornwall Gazette,* 17th March 1804) that appeared in Cornwall. It is an account which must have occasioned consternation and anxiety in the minds of the steward and staff at Boconnoc. I begin it after the insult in the coffee house had been made:

> ... High words followed. Mr Best left the room and sent his lordship a challenge. Notice of the affair was immediately sent off by the Master of the Coffee-house to the Police Offices, and the runners were despatched in quest of the parties.
>
> Lord Camelford's and Mr Best's lodgings were watched all night but the parties eluded their vigilance by sleeping out.

The antagonists, with their seconds, met on ground close to Holland Park.

> On the ground Mr Best is said to have entreated his lordship to make some concession, by revoking the offensive expressions made use of in the coffee-room, in answer to which his lordship said, 'Mr Best, I do not come here to be trifled with; take your ground and prepare yourself;' the ground had been previously marked out. They then took their distance, and it was agreed by the seconds they should fire together.
>
> It is said that his lordship's pistol was fired first without effect, and Mr Best's immediately after. When Lord C. fell, Mr B. ran up and said, 'Camelford, I hope you are not seriously hurt.' His lordship replied, 'I suspect I am, but I forgive you'. Mr Best rejoined, 'Again I declare I am innocent of the charge you made against me'. Lord C. replied, 'I believe you are not to blame, but you had better provide for

your safety' [by fleeing before the Police arrived].

Mr Best and his seconds then left his lordship on the ground, went to a post-chaise and four, which was waiting at the bottom of the lane, and instantly rode off.

The man belonging to hammersmith turnpike witnessed the rencontre and on the departure of the persons concerned, came up and said to Lord C., 'Shall I get assistance and pursue them?' His Lordship said, 'No, help me up.' Lord C. was then taken to Mr Ottey's house which is about a hundred yards from the spot where the unfortunate event took place. His lordship was immediately put to bed, and a surgeon was sent for. Lord C. was for a time insensible and much convulsed from the pain . . . .

The ball had entered below the right rib, and penetrated nearly through the body inclining downwards. It is supposed to be lodged in the loins near the backbone and to have carried a piece of the flannel waistcoat along with it.

His lordship lay in extreme torture the whole of Wednesday . . . . . on Thursday he had some repose, and gave orders to one of his servants to go to Hampstead to fetch some things he had left there . . . . . .

There were many persons who applied to see his lordship, but his medical attendants refused permission to all, except his lordship's particular friend, Mr James Cockburn. During the night he lost the use of his legs and thighs, and his kidneys ceased to function. From these events no hopes were entertained that he could survive many hours longer . . . . . .

Lord and Lady Grenville arrived on Thursday afternoon from Dropmore. Lady Grenville (Camelford's sister) was in deep distress; her attachment for her brother being very strong from their infancy. On her Ladyship's entering the house she nearly fainted away, in consequence of which it was not deemed proper for her to see her brother in his present state. Lord Grenville was present at a consultation with his surgeons that lasted nearly two hours.

Lord Camelford hung on to the Saturday before he died, and on the Monday was the Coroner's inquest to which witnesses gave a more detailed account of the events at the duel:

The principal witness was James Sheers, Gardener to Lord Holland, who stated that on Wednesday morning last he was at work at Lord Holland's digging in the shrubbery, when he heard the report of two pistols. He told the man at work with him (John Murray) that he thought it was a duel. He ran down to the pales adjoining the field and saw the smoke in the second field, about ten yards distant from the hedge. He observed the deceased lying on the ground and a person, the second, supporting him. The witness ran down and there were two other gentlemen coming from Lord Camelford.

The gentleman supporting Lord C. called to the witness to come and help ... The deceased begged very hard of the witness to help him, accordingly he took hold of the cape of his coat and the gentleman who had been supporting him ran for a surgeon. Before this the witness had, at the request of this gentleman, instructed two of his labourers to go and stop two men who were now some distance away, but this they had not been able to do.

Soon after Surgeon Thompson coming, the deceased asked the witness why he called out to stop the gentlemen? He went on to say he did not wish to have them stopped, that he was the aggressor, that he forgave the gentleman who had shot him, and he hoped God would forgive him, too.

In five or six minutes several other persons came to his assistance. The witness asked the deceased whether he knew his friend, or any of the opposition party? And the answer was that, 'He knew nothing, he was a dead man'. The remainder of Lord Holland's gardeners came up: a chair was sent for, Lord C. was put in it and carried to Mr Ottey's. The witness got the deceased upstairs and helped to put him to bed; his neck-cloth was taken off and his shirt pulled over, when he appeared to have received a wound in his right shoulder. He saw no pistol.

The jury returned a verdict that the deceased had been killed by a person or persons unknown.

There are two further items of news in this copy of the *Royal Cornwall Gazette*. The first is an account of a typical display of high spirits by Lord Camelford, heedless of the possible consequences to other people. It was the occasion of a bet between him and Best made in the coffee house only a few days before. It is certainly a display of a gambler's lust for thrill:

> The parties a few days before [writes the *Gazette,*] at the same Coffee-house in Conduit Street where the quarrel originated. After dinner, Mr Best proposed to his Lordship to shoot with a pistol at a mark, and to pit his blood mare against a sum of one hundred guineas. Lord Camelford agreed: he was to fire three times at a lighted candle placed on a table at ten yards' distance, and if his lordship put it out once in three times, he was to win the mare, Lord C.'s second fire took off the snuff of the candle, and in the third he broke the candle, but not succeeding in putting it out, he lost the wager.

Lord Camelford was only twenty-nine when he died, and Boconnoc passed appropriately into the more stable ownership of the Grenvilles, the estate living happily ever since.

III

The Saint in Golden Cuthbert Mayne

Viewed from *Spray*, a mile offshore, the cliffs on either side of Mawgan Porth are uncompromising in their lofty assurance of their belonging. 'Nobody to enter here,' they seem to growl, 'nobody without our approval.'

The beach which they embrace on either side is a place for children to splash and swim, for girls to display the joys of youth, for young golden gods, with long fair hair and clear blue eyes and bronzed skin, to ride the waves, deftly, on surfboards.

The long white tumbling breakers seem to smile in the company of those who sport in their pummelling liveliness. On a summer's day, with sun shining, and friendly white cumulus clouds sailing by like galleons against the sky, the white surf of the waves happily envelops in spray the holiday-makers cavorting and laughing as they wipe the salt from their eyes.

As I visualise this holiday scene while standing up in the bows of *Spray* as we slowly sail by, my mind is fixed on a contrast, on the winter scene, on ships in trouble, helpless in an onshore gale to escape destruction on the rocks either side.

Particularly I see in my mind a spectacular photograph of one such wreck, of the *Hodbarrow Miner*, from Runcorn with coal to Truro. She came ashore on 2nd March 1908 after a tremendous fight lasting many hours, but finally succumbed and grounded, broadside on to the waves in the stormy maelstrom of Mawgan Porth. All but one of her crew were lost.

She holds a particular place in my mind, for her sturdy mainmast now lies on ground not two hundred yards from where I write, a reminder of the power of the sea.

Just a mile or so up the valley whose mouth opens out at Mawgan Porth, is the village of St Mawgan. Here it is a different world, a gentle place remote in character from that of its namesake by the sea. Here now is the green leafy setting at the foot of the lush slopes of the narrow valley; here is the stream winding its way under a stone bridge, and through a placid meadow; here is the old pub, and the lovely fourteenth century church, on land where there had been a place of worship through a thousand years before that.

Close to the old church is the manor house, Lanherne, set back from the road and only just allowing the visitor to the village a glimpse, through the trees and foliage, of its ancient face, but is enough for him to feel the peace and tranquillity that dwells within.

Since the end of the eighteenth century, when Lanherne was given by one of the last of Arundells as sanctuary to sixteen nuns fleeing from persecution during the French Revolution, it has been a convent for the enclosed Order of Carmelites. It thus continues the strong Catholic tradition of the house and the family which was bravely maintained throughout the Reformation and the dangerous years for Catholics that followed.

Preserved closely within the convent are sacred relics from this stormy period, one of which is a portion of the skull of one of the many martyrs at that time, Cuthbert Mayne. It is of this man that I am thinking as I now loll, all too comfortably, in the cockpit of *Spray* already now past the porth of Mawgan that set the story once more running in my mind.

Three hundred years back along the road of history seems to us a long way, at any rate far enough for us to dissociate ourselves from any savagery that was inflicted on the populace by the sovereign government.

But is it so long ago? Is it so far back along the road? I myself am seventy years old. *Only four of 'me's,* standing side by side represent the period in lives between now and the end of the 17th century.

With this sense of perspective in mind, consider the following 'judicial' sentence imposed by Judge Jeffreys in 1577, in the High Court, and ponder on the validity of the current view that physical violence these days is condoned more and more by society and with increasing indifference. The sentence was imposed on a man of God, whose crime was to stick to his Christian principles. Here it is:

Thou, Cuthbert Mayne, hast been here accused, for the traitorous obtaining, publishing and putting in use of a printed instrument containing matter of absolution from the See of Rome, [this he wholly denied] contrary to the laws of this land, and hast thereunto pleaded, Not Guilty; and for trial thereof hast put thyself upon God and the country, who have found thee guilty.

The Court therefore doth award that thou shalt be carried from hence unto the place from whence thou camest and from thence thou shalt be drawn into the market place of this town [Launceston] where thou shalt be hanged until thou be half dead. . . . . .and thy bowels be taken out of thy body, and before thy face, being still alive, shall be thrown into the fire, and then thy head shall be cut off and thy body divided into four parts to be hanged up in several places as the Queen's Majesty shall appoint [Bodmin, Barnstaple, Tregony and Wadebridge]; and so God have mercy on your soul.

In 1878 there was published in London a five hundred page volume, in Latin and English, of the first and second Diaries of the English College in Douai, France, in 1568. I shall be referring in more detail to this college, a supreme act of faith if ever there was one, and which was established for no less purpose than to replace the function of the disbanded monasteries in England so far as training priests was concerned. It was a college for volunteer priests, to be trained and then put secretly back into England.

The editor of this tome was Thomas Francis Knox D.D., and he also wrote the historical introduction which includes a concise picture of the complex period which saw the almost total eclipse of Catholic worship in England under Queen Elizabeth. No Mass could be held anywhere on pain of death for those responsible or life imprisonment for those partaking.

The college of Douai was very largely responsible for filling a vacuum with brave newly ordained priests smuggled across the Channel, each conscious that he was almost certainly to be discovered only to die a martyr's death. The wonderful faith this reflected was shown by the veritable eagerness with which volunteers crossed into France for their instruction at Douai, the prospect of their capture on their return to England and hideous death providing for them the grace of companionship with Christ on the Cross.

It was at this time that the Catholic light in England was all but extinguished but it was rescued and nourished in time by the initiative of Douai, an initiative that has its visible effect today when, in spite of the media talking of empty churches when they mean Protestant or non-comformist churches, the Catholic faith in England is reflected in full churches, and, in a holiday town I know, with sometimes as many as six Masses in one day, with an overflow in the garden.

Yes, those were dangerous times, and for a quick résumé of the setting that led to them, I shall draw on the accounts of Knox in his introduction to the Diaries, and from John Morris's *Troubles of our Catholic Forefathers*, 1872. I ask the reader, who may feel himself an outsider so far as any interest in religion in such a period is concerned, to stay with me for I am sure he will find the facts that led to the persecution in our green and pleasant land to be intiguing in their evil logic and ruthlessness, and will think that the power that authority had over the people then, motivated by fear and self-interest, may not be so very far away from us today.

On Elizabeth ascending the throne in 1558, she was determined to cut England off from the unity of the original church of Catholic Christendom. To do this she was resolved, no matter at what cost, to impose upon her subjects a new religion which would free her from the knowledge and experience of having a large proportion of her subjects retaining their loyalty to the Pope. The Pope, it must be remembered, was also the spiritual head of her enemies in Europe. Philip of Spain was threatening invasion. It was intolerable that English soldiers and sailors should have such a strong link with the enemy. No security from traitors in her midst could be assured unless the link, membership of the Catholic church, was severed. That was her reasoning, surely understandable.

Elizabeth's motives for religious persecution in England were therefore political, whereas the reasons for priests defying the law and, in hiding, continuing to say Mass, were wholly religious.

The Queen and her advisers were fully aware that what they proposed for themselves was difficult and perilous, but they never doubted ultimate success and they had no scruples about the way they were going to get their way. However, they knew that they would only be able to attain their end by caution and patience.

The successive changes in the established religion that had taken place one after another during three successive reigns without causing commotion pointed to the indifference in which religious affairs appeared to be held in the country.

On the other hand, the way the mass of people returned to the Catholic church in Mary's reign was fairly recent evidence that the ancient faith still held a warm place in the hearts of the majority though they were too frightened to strive for its maintenance.

As things turned out, it was only by a slender majority, skilfully obtained by playing upon the hopes, fears and religious indifference of the peers that Elizabeth was able to undo her late sister's work, and to separate England once again from the Catholic church.

Heavy, sweeping penalties were now prescribed, and the new gospel imposed upon all her subjects. The Queen's government passed appropriate statutes for this purpose in 1559 and 1563, but the measures prescribed were found to be insufficient.

Elizabeth and her Ministers had hoped that a few years of such repression would extinguish the Faith in England, as it had been extinguished in Sweden, Denmark and Norway, but it was not so.

In England, there were now no bishops except those in prison, no churches, no monasteries, no Catholic institutions for charity or education. The preaching of the word of God for Catholics existed no longer except secretly in holes and corners.

In 1563 Elizabeth introduced a new penal statute that matched infringement of the laws of the previous statutes with high treason, and carrying the same grievous penalties, including death in the manner I have already indicated. The situation that faced the Catholic was clear. Anyone who denied that the Queen was Supreme Head on earth of the Church of England was committing high treason, to be punished with the foregoing appalling penalties, according to the law. In fact, he was invoking martyrdom.

But the Catholic religion, however, required the faithful to deny this usurped spiritual supremacy of the Queen. It was the Pope, not the Queen, who was Spiritual Head, and a Catholic committed a grievous sin against the Faith if he said otherwise.

No wonder Catholics were lying low, but how wonderful it was the Seminary in Douai, mentioned earlier, had no shortage of young volunteers coming from England to learn, to qualify, and then to return to minister in such enemy territory as England. Their motive was in the true name of love, love for Christ, love for their fellow men and for this they joyously offered their lives. They embraced the fellowship of pain, the sufferings of Christ being the banner that drew them. The opportunity to share Christ's agony was the way to come closer to him, to be worthy of his love, to share the pain, to share the glory. Such was their faith.

It was the fifteenth of these missionaries sent from Douai whom God chose to be the first martyr, of many, from the Seminary. Cuthbert Mayne was himself a convert. He was born in 1544 at Goulston, in the parish of Sherwell, near Barnstaple and was brought up a Protestant by an elderly uncle. When Cuthbert was nineteen his uncle got him ordained a minister. Later he confessed that at the time he had no idea what ministry or religion meant.

Educated at Barnstaple School, Mayne now went to Oxford, becoming in due course chaplain of the newly established College of St John. Throughout his period in this post Cuthbert Mayne was an unhappy man. He was a troubled man for he felt himself more and more despising himself for his insincerity in not complying with his conscience by confessing his growing conviction of the truth of the Catholic faith. Further to his distress, he could not bring himself to overcome the poverty he dreaded and which he would have to face if he threw up his appointment at St John's. He shrank, too, from the loss of his friends.

Cuthbert Mayne therefore remained as he was, all the while grieving for the error, if not the sin, in which he had lived, wretched over the profane office which he continued to hold, and yearning to acclaim the truth of the Holy Church.

Fortunately, Mayne was a most likable fellow and at Oxford he was making many friends of all persuasions. Two of these Gregory Martin and Edmund Campion (later one of the first to be martyred) had taken the bold action he envied and had given up friends, country and worldly prospects and were now studying at the Douai Seminary. From here they wrote letters to their vacillating friend still at Oxford entreating him to break away and follow them.

One of these letters fell into the hands of the Bishop of London, and serious in its implications though it was, it freed Mayne's conscience at last and forced him, albeit after a delay, to face the facts, for the Bishop on making this discovery of the state of mind of the chaplain of St John's and others named in the letter, sent to have them arrested.

They were all seized and thrown into prison, except Cuthbert Mayne who was away and was at once warned of his danger by his friend at Oxford, Thomas Ford, a fellow of Trinity College and later also a martyr. The date of this is thought to be 1570, not earlier, as Thomas Ford in that year was admitted into the Seminary at Douai. It was two or three years later that at last Cuthbert Mayne made his way from somewhere on the Cornish coast to the Continent. In 1573 his arrival in Douai is registered in the College Diaries. He was at once admitted into the Seminary by its Head, Dr Allen, and there applied himself wholeheartedly to the study of theology and holiness.

It is of interest to learn of the work and atmosphere of the Seminary, and we are lucky to have a report on the spiritual training and studies pursued at this time, and I think that extracts I will take from the account in Allen's own words on his return there after eight months in Rome, will not be the pious platitudes the humanists among my readers might expect. Rather, I think, it must interest anyone who has an ear for the unusual and a cheer for the courageous whatever the cause.

Allen found everything flourishing with over a hundred students in the College, and he wrote;

> Great have been the difficulties of our temporal administration, especially at the present time, when owing to the cruel laws made in England against those who aid us, we have been forced to live almost entirely on the Pope's allowance, though the college has never of late years had fewer than 100 students of whom 20 to 25 are priests and the rest candidates for holy order [to be sent to England risking their lives as missionaries when ordained].

In ordinary years we advance to the priesthood twenty or thereabouts and send as many every year to England. Since the college began we have given to the Lord's work above 160 priests, concerning whose instruction, learning and method of training ...... is as follows.

Our students being intended for the English harvest are not required to excel or be great proficients in theological science though their teachers ought to be as learned and prudent as possible; but they must abound in zeal for God's house, Charity, and thirst for souls ...... When they have burning zeal, even though deep science be wanting, provided they always know the necessary heads of religious doctrine and the power and nature of the sacraments, such men among the more skilled labourers whom we have in nearly all the provinces of the kingdom, also do good work hearing confessions and offering sacrifice ......

Moreover, we make it our first and foremost study, both in the seminary and in England by means of our labourers, to stir up, so far as God permits, in the minds of Catholics a zealous and just indignation against the heretics ......

We picture to them by mournful contrast [the majesty of ceremonial here and elsewhere than England] the utter desolation at home, of all things sacred which there exists, our country once so famed for its religion and holy before God, now void of all religion, our friends and dear ones, our kinsfolk, all our dear ones and countless souls besides perishing in schism and godlessness, every jail and dungeon filled to overflowing, not with thieves and villains, but with Christ's priests and servants, nay, with our parents and kinsmen ...

Allen goes on and says, 'Then turning to ourselves we must needs confess that all these things have come upon our country through our sins. ...' and then he extols on what they should do about it, after which he writes in more detail of the curriculum.

I ask the reader's further indulgence, however uninterested he believes himself to be in theology, to stay with me a little while longer on this theme of study; for the sincerity of its purpose, and the risks facing the student in fulfilling that purpose, cannot fail to arouse one's repect and fascination for their sublime endeavour.

It was considered of first importance that they should be very familiar with the text of Holy Scripture and have at their finger-tips all the passages that could be used to counter accusations from the heretics. Thus there was a daily lecture on the New Testament in which the exact sense of the words was dictated to them. Then everyday at table after dinner and after supper and before they left their places, they heard a running explanation of one chapter of the old and another of the new Testament.

At suitable times during the day instruction on the controversies of the day was given, and notes taken on the arguments to expect from heretics anxious to distort the true meaning. Once a week a 'disputation' was held on these passages of Scripture, in which the students defended in turn not only the Catholic side against the texts of Scripture but also the heretical side. The masters present never allowed anything to be passed over by either side without its being submitted to thorough examination. This was followed by one of the students making a continuous discourse, as though it were a sermon, directed to persuade his hearers. This took place twice a week.

The Bible was always read at dinner and supper, and with close attention. Usually four, or at least three, chapters were read followed by a portion of church history or martyrology (history of martyrs). Everything read at table had to have been studied in his own room by each student beforehand.

In this way, the Old Testament was gone through twelve times every three years which was the usual duration of a student at the college. The New Testament was read through sixteen times in the same period. Not surprisingly, this was considered 'a great help towards acquiring a more than common familiarity with the text'.

An interesting feature in the curriculum was that 'by frequent and friendly conversations we make our students thoroughly acquainted with the chief impieties, blasphemies, absurdities, cheat and trickeries of the English heretics, as well as with their ridiculous writings, sayings and doings . . .'

In the course of 1575, Doctor Allen had Cuthbert Mayne ordained, and on 24th April the following year (1576), with the blessing of his Superior and the prayers of his colleagues, he left the coast of France for the sullen shores of England. Accompanying him was another missionary for whom the future also held martyrdom. He was John Payne.

It is edifying at this point to think of those other heroes, those modern heroes who crossed the Channel, too, but in the other direction four hundred years later, secretly and in darkness, those British and French Secret Agents who, like Mayne, were willing to sacrifice themselves that the truth might triumph.

After anxious moments in stormy weather off the coast of England, and doubts as to the most likely port or haven where they might slip in unnoticed, the two priests set foot in England. Almost immediately they separated. They were to meet again only when they had each 'won the martyr's palm'.

Two items of news reached the Seminary a few weeks later, on 28th June. One was that the heretics were evidently astonished and infuriated on account of the number of conversions that were being made, and all kinds of tortures were being threatened against anyone, layman or priest, who was caught in such illegal actions designated by the Queen, as we have seen, as high treason.

After a short visit to his native Devonshire, Cuthbert Mayne went to live in the house of Francis Tregian, at Golden near Probus and five miles from Truro. Tregian, pronounced 'Trudgeon', was a man with a large estate and a fortune made in the mining of Cornish tin. Golden was off the beaten track, as good a place as could be found for a missionary to shelter, for Mr Tregian was hospitable, courageous and a fervent Catholic.

This was the normal way for the missionaries to act so as to perform their task with least chance of surprise and capture. Within the estate of an influential family with a large household they were, though at risk, able to say Mass, preach and administer the Sacraments to the neighbouring Catholics, and they could also find many opportunities for meeting those whose conversion was thought to be hopeful.

Alas, within a few months, vague rumours were spread about and the storm, which was always hovering in the vicinity, suddenly became near and violent, and broke over Golden, the Tregian house.

On 8th June 1577, the Bishop of Exeter was making a visitation at Truro, when he decided to satisfy his anti-Catholic hatred by investigating a rumour that had come to his ears that all was not loyal at Golden. The historically famous and admired Sir Richard Grenville (later to die in the *Revenge*) was High Sheriff, and no doubt he was eager to agree when the request for a search to be made of Golden reached him at Stowe on the morning probably of 7th June.

Accordingly, unknown to the owner of Golden and his guest, a formidable posse of men were on the march to surprise them. Headed by the Sheriff of the county himself, it included nine Justices of the Peace, and well over a hundred people.

Before we hear them hammer on the door of this quiet and sheltered mansion, well off the main track and standing amid one of the more gentle of Cornish landscapes, let us consider for a moment the kind of life style of their quarry whom they hoped to obtain.

Cuthbert Mayne was, for the moment and while he was at Golden, better off than most missionaries, but he, and each of them, had to endure the constant need for alertness, for the restraint from all natural freedom, and with the anxiety, punctuated by fear that could never be absent for long; for this was enemy territory and every applicant for conversion could be an agent planted by the foe.

We have a letter, included in the Douai Diaries, written a little later, it is true, but giving an idea of the restrictions and doubts any one of the secret missionaries in England was having to undergo.

The letter is from Doctor Allen, the learned Head of the Seminary, to Maurice Channey, formerly of the London Charterhouse and at this time prior of the English Carthusians at Bruges.

> This is certain, that priests [in England] had need to pray instantly and fast much, and watch and ward themselves well lest the needless use of sundry enticements to sin and necessary dissimulation in things of themselves indifferent, to be fit for every company, bring them to offend God, and so while they labour to save others themselves become reprobate.
>
> Wherein they must also be more careful of their ways, for that every man's eyes be cast upon them as on such as take upon them to be guides of other men's lives and belief.

I could reckon unto you the miseries they suffer on night journies in the worst weather that can be picked, peril of thieves, of waters, of watches, of false brethren; their close abode in chambers as in prison or dungeon without fire or candle lest they give token to the enemy where they be; their often and sudden rising from their beds at midnight to avoid the diligent searches of heretics, all which and divers other discontentments, disgraces and reproaches they willingly suffer, which is great penance for their feathers [secular disguises]; and all to win the souls of their dearest countrymen which pains few men pity as they should do, and not many reward them as they ought to do.

Now it was Cuthbert Mayne who was about to sense the chill feel of possible discovery. Before him lay an ordeal of horrific proportions, throughout which he never lost his dignity and poise. But on this day, 8th June 1577, he was unaware of the arrival of the sinister party, he being somewhere from which the sound of horses approaching and voices at the front door could not be heard.

However Tregian heard, and he met them on the threshold. The High Sheriff announced to him that word had been received that a man called Bourne, from London, who had committed an offence for which he was wanted, had taken refuge in Golden. 'We require to search the house,' he said, and forthwith signalled for his men to come in. Several entered while Tregian protested that no such person was in the house and that he had no idea where he might be. He went on to protest against the indignity of searching a gentleman's house without a warrant from the Queen.

Resistance to such a force was impossible, and Sir Richard Grenville, with dagger drawn and making threats of violence, forced his way into the house with his followers.

Cuthbert Mayne was still completely unaware of what was going on. Then, coming into his room by the garden entrance, and hearing the battering on his other door, which was locked, opened it and found himself face to face with the High Sheriff. To the latter's sharp enquiry as to who he was, he replied quietly, 'I am a man'. Grenville ordered him to be searched. Almost immediately the searcher triumphantly handed Grenville Mayne's necklace from which was suspended hidden beneath his shift, a small silver and crystal medallion with an emblem on it. It was enough. It was all Grenville wanted. It was an Agnus Dei, enough to convict a man of high treason from the Act of 1571.

The relevant Section included the following: 'If anyone shall bring into the realm any token or thing called by the name Agnus Dei, or any crosses, pictures, beads or such like thing from the Bishop of Rome, or any person claiming authority from the Bishop of Rome to conscrate or hallow them.'

Without any delay, the priest was taken off to the Bishop of Exeter in Truro, and there followed after him the books and papers that had been in his possession.

Francis Tregian was unhappily arrested, too, but was later freed for a short time before he was re-arrested, and his appalling experiences in captivity began; but this is another story.

After seeing the Bishop and being questioned, Mayne was taken to Launceston and confined in a dark and filthy underground dungeon. Heavy irons were fixed to his legs and he was allowed nothing to read, nor was he given a candle.

The capture was regarded as very important, and, indeed, that is understandable if one relates it to attitudes in the Second World War when the finding of a Swastika badge on an Englishman who was hiding would have been quite enough to take him to be at least a Nazi sympathiser, if not spy. With Catholic Spain our enemy, waiting for an opportunity to invade us, it was understandable that Grenville should have treated Mayne as a potential enemy. His link as a Catholic with Spain through loyalty to the Pope superseded his loyalty to Elizabeth. Spain fought with two weapons, the gun and the rosary; if you go to the museum at Penzance you can see there a ship's cannon from a Spanish warship with an embossed rosary on the barrel which neatly establishes the point.

Eight days after the arrest, on 16th June (it might have been 16th September) the Assizes commenced at Launceston. The Earl of Bedford was among those present, and Cuthbert Mayne was brought to trial, together with Francis Tregian (brought back from London where he had been held) and several local gentlemen and servants who were accused of aiding and abetting. In an attempt to humiliate them, the prisoners were made to stand at the bar with their outer clothing removed.

An elaborate indictment was read against the prisoner which included the following accusations, all of which were denied by Mayne and the prisoners.

1. That he had on a certain day traitorously obtained from the Roman See a printed faculty [the Pope's Jubilee edict] containing matter of absolution of sundry subjects of the kingdom.
2. That on a day named he had traitorously published the said document at Golden.
3. That on another day he had at Launceston maliciously and with evil intent taught and defended, in express words, the ecclesiastical power of a foreign Bishop, to wit, the Bishop of Rome, heretofore usurped in this kingdom [taken over by].
4. That on a certain day he had brought into this kingdom a vain and superstitious thing called an Agnus Dei, blessed, as they say, by the said Bishop of Rome, and had delivered the same to Mr Francis Tregian.
5. That on a day named he had publicly said Mass and administered the Lord's Supper according to the Popish right, and all these things contrary to statutes made in the 1st and 13th years of our sovereign lady Queen Elizabeth and against her peace and crown and dignity.

I do not propose to go into the trial at any length, but I would ask the reader to imagine himself to be one of the Jury listening to Sir John Popham, the Queen's attorney, opening his case.

After repeating the foregoing charges in greater detail than I have outlined, he begins his address to the Jury.

Masters, you that are sworn, you have heard by the indictment, which hath been here read unto you, how this man Cuthbert Mayne, hath obtained from the See of Rome a certain Bull, being an instrument of absolution which they call a Jubilee, and within the Queen's dominions here hath published, and put the same in use, contrary to a statute made in the thirteenth year of the Queen's reign, and that these men, knowing he did so, have aided and maintained him contrary to the said statute.

And further you have heard how, contrary to another statute, by express words he hath maintained the usurped power and authority of the Bishop of Rome, and they likewise have maintained and comforted him. You have also heard how he likewise offered an Agnus Dei unto Francis Tregian, Esquire, his master, and that these men, also knowing the same, have concealed the offer.

And lastly, you have heard how he hath said Mass, contrary also to another statute made in the Queen's reign, unto all which indictments they have severally pleaded not guilty, and for trial thereof have put themselves before God and the country, *which be you.*

So your charge is this: to inquire whether they be guilty or no. First, concerning the Bull, to prove that Cuthbert Mayne hath obtained and put the same in use, you must note that he is a Priest who came lately from Rome, and brought this Bull with him (showing a copy of the Jubilee printed at Douai) which was found in his chamber and he cannot deny it.

Now the effect of this instrument is to give a Priest authority to absolve sinners, and he being a Priest is come hither for that purpose, and thereby hath brought his master [Tregian] and the most part of his servants and divers others here present, into a certain obstinacy against the Queen's proceedings whereby they do refuse to frequent the Divine Service now used [made compulsory by law] and doth thereby harden the hearts of the Queen's subjects against her, intending, no doubt, to move some rebellion within this realm ......

The trial made no pretence at seeking to do justice. The most elementary principles of evidence and argument were violated, but such were the morals of the times. That may be difficult to imagine from this distance when now there seems to be no lack of rights and freedom societies who are ready to pounce on justice as prejudice if it dares to convict a terrorist or a policeman's armed assailant.

During the case Cuthbert Mayne tried to convince the court of the truth, that the Bull did not come from Rome, that he had not come from Rome but from Douai where it was printed, nor had he ever published it at Golden or anywhere else. No evidence had been offered of the alleged publication, or that the Agnus Dei had been brought from Rome, or that he had brought it into England, or that he had given it to Francis Tregian.

It was not proof that he had said Mass, he argued, just because they had found his missal, chalice and vestments in his room.

At one stage, during the course of one of Cuthbert Mayne's calm attempts to deny the charges, one of the Judges, Sir Roger Manwood interrupted him, and turning to the jury he made the following argument which was typical of the standard of so-called justice that the Court was applying.

Judge Manwood said,

> Masters, you that are sworn, this fellow here, Cuthbert Mayne, is, as you see, a Rome-runner, a secret traitor to the Queen and her realm, and one that goeth about to seduce people from their obedience both to God and to their Prince, and therefore is to have no favour at all.
>
> Wherefore, for your better instruction, you must remember that, in causes where direct proofs cannot be had, there presumpsions must be allowed; for if a man be murdered, and a murderer found with a bloody weapon in his hand, and his clothes all bloody, this is such a presumpsion, although he were not seen to commit the murder, as amounted to a just and perfect proof.

And then the judge said,

> But, much more, treasons are *always* tried out by presumpsions, or otherwise traitors would never be known.
>
> So therefore this man, having this Bull with him in his custody, coming from Douai and other countries, as himself confesseth, beyond the seas, being also a very lewd fellow, and refusing to come to the church [of England], and to obey the Queen's most Godly proceedings, is, therefore, without all doubt, manifestly convinced, as guilty to the several treasons laid to his charge.

The jury, after deliberating some time, were still undecided, in spite of the strongly prejudiced direction. This delay obviously was unexpected and very vexing for the accusers, and one of them, the High Sheriff himself, went amongst them and held a long consultation with them, an act that was wholly illegal then as it would be now. It is hardly surprising that the jury succumbed to his blandishments and pronounced Cuthbert Mayne guilty of high treason. Tregian and the other accused they found guilty of felony.

The next day, they were all brought up again for sentence. Cuthbert Mayne was alone at their head, while the others were coupled two together with iron chains. Mayne had his arms and hands fettered with irons. This woeful little procession moved as well as they could from the gaol to the court, rousing much admiration of those who saw them pass so calmly.

On hearing his sentence, Cuthbert Mayne 'raised his eyes and hands to heaven, and with a calm face and joyful countenance' cried aloud, 'Deo gratias!'

Then he was taken back to his dark dungeon in Launceston Castle. He was to remain there in isolation for the next five months.

This long delay was due to the fact that a difference of opinion rose over the case between the two judges of the Assizes. Judge Jeffreys had allowed himself to be overborne by Manwood, and subsequently forwarded to the Privy Council a Report of the trial and his reasons for not concurring in the sentence. By order of the Council, the case was dismissed by all the judges, nominated by the Council, together, but they were as little agreed as the first two, though the judges of greater authority took the side of Jeffreys.

The Government, however, was only too well aware of the stream of missionaries that were coming into the country and they were not in the mood for compromise, were furious over the success that the missionaries were having ('stung by the abundant fruits of their apostolate', wrote John Morris). In the end, an order was sent to the High Sheriff, signed by eight Privy Councillors, to proceed with the execution.

When Cuthbert Mayne was told that he was to die in three days, he responded in a way that no one without the gift of faith would think was anything but purple prose on the part of the reporter; but the wonder of God-given faith is that a martyr's sacrifice of himself for Christ is entirely comprehensible to the committed Christian, who sees it as a call of close fellowship with Christ on the Cross. He shares with him the agony as well as the glory.

Yes, so let us hear what Cuthbert Mayne said when faced with this news. He said to the bearer of it that he heartily thanked him, and said he would most gladly have rewarded him had he (Mayne) anything to give, since he was the first to bring him such joyful news.

From that moment, the martyr gave himself up to more intimate prayer and preparation for his passion.

The day before his execution he was brought out of his prison to a conference with a number of dignitaries and others who had come with two ministers to see him. Then began for him a marathon unofficial cross-examination that lasted from eight in the morning until nightfall. Loaded with heavy irons, as he was, and weakened by months of prison treatment, he was the equal of them all in stamina and argument, his faith and constancy being never shaken.

The lawyers and others among the 'inquisitors' were impressed, and did their best to persuade the martyr to think again. They assured him they could answer for his life and liberty if only he would affirm on oath that the Queen was the Supreme Head of the Church in England. There was a pause. Then Cuthbert Mayne asked for a Bible, and for a moment those present thought that fear of death and desire for life had prevailed.

The martyr took the Bible, kissed it, made the sign of the Cross and then spoke clearly and firmly. He said to the assembled company, 'The Queen never was, nor is, nor ever shall be, the head of the Church of England.'

Here I should like to mention for those not conversant with the ecclesiastical status in the British Constitution that the Catholic Church was the Church of England until Henry VIII and the Reformation. Since then, the Queen has been head of the Protestant and other churches, but historically the Catholics have remained as they have been since Peter was charged with the task of being head of the Church. The Popes in their long unbroken line of succession from him, have kept it thus.

If it had not been for those men and women whom we've been considering, brave upholders of the Catholic faith through all the noise of political axes that have been ground unsuccessfully to fell it, then the Supreme Pontiff, the Pope, would have had none of his 750,000,000 world flock in England, and there would have been no Catholics to fill their churches to overflowing as they do today.

The day of execution dawned. It was 30th November 1577, a market day. The martyr was led out of his cell and was made ready for the first stage of his ordeal, which was to bind him to the hurdle which would be drawn swiftly by horses over the rough road. The gibbet in the market place was very high with a ladder against it which he was made to climb up backwards. Awkwardly poised on the ladder he was told to say a few words. In his speech he referred his case to the judgement of Almighty God and made a strong plea for Francis Tregian, saying he was unaware of all things of which he himself had been accused.

Beginning on another theme, one of the justices interrupted him commanding the hangman to put the rope about his neck saying he could preach afterwards. Then Sir Reginald Mohun, of Boconnoc, ordered the ladder to be overturned, so that he had not the time to finish the verse he had just started, *In manes tuas Domine* . . .

He was cut down almost immediately and the height of his fall injured him badly. He was swinging by his neck when he was cut down, and the force of the swing caused his head to strike the scaffold 'which was there prepared of purpose to divide the quarters, as the one side of the face was very sorely bruised, and one of his eyes far driven out of his head.

'After he was cut down the hangman first spoiled him of his clothes . . . . . . and then in butcherly manner opening his belly he rent up his bowels, and after tore out his heart, the which as a plausible spectacle he held up aloft in his hand, showing it unto the people; lastly, his head was cut off, and his body divided into four quarters . . . . . .' These were distributed in the manner I earlier indicated, but the significance of one quarter being displayed in Tregony is that Tregony is within a mile or so of Golden, Francis Tregian's house.

And the martyr's head? Surely the heretical ritual decreed that the head was the most potent relic of all and worthy of gruesome display? Yes, they did. It was hoisted on a pike at Launceston, then taken to a place on the bridge at Wadebridge.

Many, many years later, in 1807, the whereabouts of the skull became known when Mr Richard Rawe brought the crown of the skull back to Lanherne as a present to the Carmelite Community. I say 'back to Lanherne' for a good reason. Mr Rawe was a descendant of Bridget Arundell of Trevithick who had been, it is believed, its guardian since one of the Arundells of Lanherne, Thomas, nephew of Sir John, had seized it from off the pike and galloped home with it to Lanherne.

This venerable relic of the martyr clearly shows where the point of the pike penetrated, and shares a sacred place in the Convent to this day in company with Cuthbert Mayne's chalice and an old black book.

Edmund Campion, the friend of Mayne at Douai who coaxed him to break his bonds with St Mary's at Oxford and join the Seminary, did not hear of his martyrdom until a year had gone by.

Shortly before he himself was martyred, he wrote to Gregory Martin from Prague this letter:

> We all thank you much for the account of Cuthbert's martyrdom. It gave many of us a real religious joy. Wretch that I am, how has that novice distanced me! May he be favourable to his old friend and tutor! I shall now boast of these titles more than ever.

Both Cuthbert Mayne, and his old friend and tutor Edmund Campion, were canonised as recently as 1970.

IV
Mr Flindell and Mr Heard

Here we are, *Spray* and I serenely sailing down this stretch of coast, between Trevose Head and Newquay, on this perfect summer afternoon. Our friendly enemy, the sea, is in amiable mood, even in loving mood, such a one as tempts me to forget that one must never take the sea for granted.

Many a small vessel has come to grief because the weather was perfect, like now, when the crew were preparing for sea, when one just cannot imagine it becoming angry maybe that very evening. Lulled by this, gear is not lashed down as it should be, hatches not secured, and emergencies not foreseen. When the storm strikes, it is no good regretting. It is too late.

Here, where we are now, such a sequence shows no signs of happening; nevertheless, all is as secure as I can make it. But have I nothing else to look out for? No, I feel I have done everything.

Then I realise I have not looked at the chart and so, putting myself in the place of a mariner a century ago, I pull out the 1859 *Channel Pilot* to see what it said of the area;

'In the way, near Mawgan Porth is a rock or two close to land, above water, and two *sunken* rocks off Mawgan Point: the outermost of these is half a mile off the point: give it therefore a wide berth in passing.' I spread out my chart, and yes, there they were. At sea, one can never be too careful, and on this same chart further evidence of victories by the friendly enemy were the emblems of wrecks peppering the offshore waters. The great cliffs were not the only hazards the mariners had to face.

And those cliffs. I look across at them, my view skimming above the gently heaving water of the ever-restless sea, and I am struck by a contrast to which they were a party: the jagged menace of the rocks at the foot, and a hundred feet above, the early summer flowers that would be in profusion. So much of Cornwall is like that, sheltered lush combes alongside wild and open ground mercilessly made barren by the ravenous gales.

In *Spray*, this day, I am enjoying on a kindly afternoon a leisurely cruise along this display of dramatic coastline. Abreast of us, for instance, is now Beacon Cove, a wonderful inlet, drying out to golden sands to which the knowledgeable make their pilgrimage, seclusion provided by its inaccessibility and the height of the encircling cliffs and the track down.

But to the mariner, Beacon Cove may look like a monster with wide open mouth ready to gollop his vessel up.

I again open my 1859 *Channel Pilot*, and read, in a footnote, of an example of the other point of view, the absence of harbours of refuge on this stretch of coast. Here it is:

> On Friday ... 1842, the brig *Erato*, 260 tons bound from Cork to Newport, with cattle, when about 40 miles SE of Cork Harbour, encountered a heavy gale of wind from NNW, and at about 2 a.m. the following morning she lost her main yard, other spars, and some canons; and running before the wind, made Trevose Head at 3.30 p.m. at which time the gale was tremendous.
>
> Not being able to weather the head, and the vessel having become ungovernable through the want of sail, she drifted towards the land.
>
> As there was not now the slightest probability of saving the vessel from destruction, the only thing thought of by the crew to save their lives was to select such a place for running her on shore as might afford some chance.
>
> When within half a mile only of Mawgan Porth, and ten minutes more would in all probability have closed the eyes of the crew in death, the master discovered a light on the western land and he bore away ......

There was another vessel in the same predicament that night. This was the *Juliana*, 200 tons, Liverpool to Torquay, and she found herself in a similar predicament, in the very same area that *Spray* and I are enjoying in comfort and safety. Both these vessels were saved from destruction at the last moment, as was explained by the two masters in a joint letter to the *Royal Cornwall Gazette* on 7th February 1843. They wrote of the unexpected light that they saw, which turned out to be Newquay harbour. 'We cannot refrain from stating it as our opinion,' they wrote, 'that there is not on the whole of the north coast of Cornwall another place where a harbour of refuge (we mean on an extended scale) would be of such importance as New Quay. The saving of life and property from such a harbour would be incalculable.'

I have mentioned that this letter appeared in the *Royal Cornwall Gazette*. This newspaper was the first in Cornwall and provided an enormous service to the mining, fishing, agricultural and shipping, as well as social, interests as a platform and disseminator of news. Until a man of courage and enthusiasm dared to start it there was no paper printed in the County.

This man was Thomas Flindell, born in Helford. It is Mr Flindell and his newspaper that we are going to meet now, and joining us later will be Mr Heard.

*

To Mr Flindell and Mr Heard, though only a minority in the county has ever heard of them, Cornwall owes much.

As rivals setting out along conflicting paths of journalism at the very beginning of this last century, they are responsible for the publication of our own two papers, printed in Cornwall every week for 170 years.

The *West Briton* is still rolling off the presses; and though the *Royal Cornwall Gazette* is no longer with us, her name is still at the masthead of the *West Briton* with whom she was merged some years ago.

To take a look at the story of these two newspapers reflects the lives of our forbears, a mirror of what made us what we are today; and you can read today, from archives holding more than a hundred and fifty years of weekly news as though they were today's.

Let us begin with the *Royal Cornwall Gazette*, and don't go away because you will be invigorated by finding yourself back in time, but still at home.

The first copy of the paper was printed and published by Thomas Flindell in Falmouth, and appeared on 7th March 1801. However, on this debut of a paper that still had its title placed before the public every week, my statement is not strictly true. The paper made its initial appearance under the title of *Cornwall Gazette and Falmouth Packet*.

Its success appeared immediate and impressive when in the nineteenth issue on 11th July, it was able to claim in capitals stretching right across the page, under the title, that it was now

CIRCULATED WITH THE UTMOST EXPEDITION THROUGH LONDON, LIVERPOOL, BATH, EXETER, PLYMOUTH AND DOCK

This was followed by a display of twenty-four parishes in Cornwall from Saltash to Falmouth, to Tregony and Camelford and 'intermediate parishes' between each of them.

On 2nd July 1803 Mr Flindell moved the publication and printing of the paper from Falmouth to Lemon St, Truro. The numbering of the paper began again with the move to Truro. Then on 17th December 1803, twenty-five issues later, the name was changed to include the 'Royal'. Polwhele, in his *History* puts the reason for these changes as being due to the fact that he had failed in the grand object of his wishes ...... 'Mr Flindell determined to make one bold effort more. From Falmouth he moved, with his wife and numerous family, to Truro, and in Truro he came out with the (*Gazette*) again.'

If that viewpoint of Polwhele's was true, Flindell showed no sign of anything but great confidence in his paper, and he was stimulated by having already ousted the *Sherborne Mercury* from its perch in Truro. In a letter to Polwhele at about this time he claimed he had a circulation there of 143, whereas the 'foreign paper' had only ten; and in the final paragraph of the 'Introduction' printed in his first Truro issue, he gives his reasons for optimism.

Claiming that the paper was favourably placed in certain directions over the London Press, he wrote,

> And we shall have some advantages ...... Much of the intelligence which the London papers derive from the South of Europe, from the West Indies, and from America, is first

brought by the packets to Falmouth. This will enable us frequently to anticipate the London papers. A correct statement of the arrival and sailing of shipping on the extensive coasts of Cornwall, with our sales of ores etc., cannot fail to excite the attention of the commercial and manufacturing towns throughout England. And when to these advantages, peculiar to the *Royal Cornwall Gazette*, we add a faithful report of the domestic affairs of the County – (which no paper printed out of the County ever did or can give) – we trust we shall be found not altogether unworthy (of) the patronage of the people of Cornwall.

Flindell's courage and enthusiasm in assuming the risks of a pioneer in a new development in Cornwall soon put him in an enviable position. He had the financial support he needed, an experienced staff by now, and this unique connection with incoming news from the outside world brought by the Packets and Naval vessels into Falmouth, where a large proportion of home-coming vessels made their first call.

A vivid example of this geographical advantage of the *Royal Cornwall Gazette* was soon to occur. One grey November morning in 1805 the naval frigate *Pickle* arrived in Falmouth haven with urgent despatches for the Admiralty from Admiral Collingwood. She was bringing the first news of the battle of Trafalgar fought and won twelve days before (23rd/24th October), together with sad tidings of the death of Nelson.

Communications being what they were it would be still more than two days before London heard the news, in person, from Lieutenant Laponetière, the frigate's captain, who set off by post chaise for the capital.

Readers of the *Sherborne Mercury* got two columns on the events, each being devoted wholly to a copy of the *London Gazette Extraordinary* of 6th November.

The *Royal Cornwall Gazette*, on the other hand, with naval contacts in its birthplace, Falmouth, was able to give an immediacy to the news which is reminiscent of the special correspondent of modern times. To supplement (if not to supplant) the handout from the Admiralty through the *London Gazette Extraordinary*, the Cornish paper was able to give news with a Truro dateline.

The *Sherborne Mercury*, even two days later and seventeen days after the battle, was limited to the official news. But the Cornish paper could present it editorially thus:

> *Truro, Saturday, November 9th.* We have this week to announce a battle more tremendous, and a conquest more glorious, than even the proud annals of the British navy could boast till now. But Lord Nelson is no more: his ardent soul departed to Heaven on the wings of Victory.
>
> The important intelligence was brought into Falmouth by the *Pickle* schooner, Lieutenant Laponentière, who proceeded immediately through Truro to London. We were therefore in hopes that last night's post could have brought us the official details of this splendid action; but there was not time for the printing of the [*London*] *Gazette* before the post left the Capital.

The writer of the paper's story was referring to the Admiralty summary (which did, in fact, arrive just before going to press) and informs his readers that it confirms all the leading features of the glorious conflict: and to these 'we shall add such other particulars as we have received through private channels'.

The subscribers, beset for years by bloody wars on the Continent, the spectre of invincible Napoleon as yet undiminished, the French and Lowland ports filled with transport and invasion expected any minute, read this eclectic news of a shattering victory in this matter.

> Lord Nelson's signal for battle was accompanied by another, which implied that 'England expected every man to do his duty.' When this was explained to several ships' crews they answered it with three cheers. The combined Fleets [French and Spanish] had added to their crews several thousand soldiers. The *Santissima Trinidada*, the largest ship in the world, carrying 146 guns and 25,000 men, was fought at close quarters and sunk by the tremendous fire of the *Victory* ... Lord Nelson was pointing out to his officers the gallant conduct of Admiral Collingwood, at the moment he received the fatal ball. He had just said, 'if we shall do our duty like Admiral Collingwood, it will be a glorious day for old

England' . . . The number of men in the enemies' fleet was treble that of the British. They have lost several thousands, and we fear the loss on our part will be found much heavier than the letter from the Admiralty indicates.

There follows another story from Plymouth, whither the *Pickle* had sailed after dropping off Laponetière at Falmouth with his despatches.

The correspondent, with information straight from 'the Admiral's Office', mainly confines himself to elaborating on the casualties. He concludes: 'Plymouth faces seem to be in mourning for the loss of our gallant and ever to be lamented Admiral; 'tis a dear bought victory.'

This astute correspondent somehow contrived to trace the recipient of a private letter from an officer in the frigate *Euryalus* to someone in Plymouth, and brought by the *Pickle*. The sense of no ordinary scoop is as alive as it was then. Dated 22nd October, it reads,

> Sir, I scarcely know whether, after so great a loss as the nation has sustained in Lord Nelson, and every one of us a friend, added to the inevitable destruction of nineteen fine prizes [wrecked in a gale on a lee shore after the battle] I ought to congratulate you – but since the enemy are *minus* so many ships, and we, I trust, not one, even in that there is matter to rejoice. Such a victory, under such circumstances so disadvantageous to the attack, never was achieved. Admiral Villeneuve [the French C-in-C] who is now at my elbow can scarcely yet credit it, and his despair and grief exceeds anything I ever saw. To resist such an attack, and seconded as Lord Nelson was, was vain. I did not leave the *Victory* till the shot were flying thick over her, and the last signal Lord Nelson made was such as cannot and never will be forgot . . . . I have no time for more – the vessel is going, but I shall soon see you as I am to carry home the Admirals.

In another letter one is given a picture of these unhappy Spanish Admirals, their lofty pride and the destruction of a supremely confidently mounted attack on England of immense proportions all laid low in one unbelievable afternoon. The letter, copy provided by the *London Gazette Extraordinary* of 6th November was from Collingwood to the Admiralty.

> I have taken Admiral Villeneuve into this ship. Vice Admiral Don Aliva is dead. Whenever the temper of the weather will permit, and I can spare a frigate ... I shall collect the other Flag Officers and send them to England with their flags (if they do not all go to the bottom), to be laid at His Majesty's feet.
>
> I am etc.
COLLINGWOOD.

By now Flindell was ensconced, and his paper was well thought of by Cornish readers for its local and political comment and news; and, too, it was in the flattering position of being in demand by London editors for its Falmouth contacts. He might, therefore, be excused for considering that his monopoly was unassailable. But, of course, it was not to be. This very monopoly fostered in a minority in Truro an increasingly active reaction to the paper's position as mouthpiece for the Government, and there grew demands for another proclaiming the new liberal force which could find expression in its columns.

At the time of the elections of 1806, still in the days of the rotten boroughs, when 44 members represented Cornwall in Parliament, there was ample opportunity for reformers to seek change. Representation in some towns was grotesque in its irrelevance. For example, Looe had the same number of MP's (four) as the City of London. Bribery of the voters was part of the scene, and only very few of the 44 MP's relied on genuine voters for their election.

The most shocking aspect from the point of view of today is, perhaps, that of the 21 Boroughs, each of which returned 2 members, 19 of them averaged but 20 eligible voters; which may have been good reason for Members not to think it worthwhile making the long journey to speak even at election time. There was thus plenty of scope for discontent among a section of the electorate, and for the critical voice to find another platform from which to urge changes.

These Reformers proved to be a body of influential men who

were in 1810 to be instrumental in forming a new paper, the *West Briton*, a paper which, within a few years was in circulation to outstrip the *Royal Cornwall Gazette*, and which one hundred and forty years later was to absorb it into its editorial bosom, allowing the while, as it is today, the daily appearance of its name to remain in the imprint of the *West Briton*. Of this I write in more detail later.

A tedious editorial slanging match was carried on by the editors of the two papers until, with the issue of 26th December 1813, Mr Flindell bowed out, and going to Exeter, became editor of the *Western Luminary*. Incidentally, Flindell's departure was signalised by an exclamatory despatch, unconfirmed from Paris, that Bonaparte had arrived in the city (from Russia). There followed a long bulletin on his retreat from Moscow, 'a tale of horror indeed. He has saved himself, but his army is lost.'

The new proprietor was Mr P. Nettleton Junior. By now the format of the front page had changed in the sense that commercial expediency had defeated the liberal display of news. Instead of the first three columns of the six available on the front page being devoted to news, they were now filled by classified advertisements of the more responsible kind, and which spilled over into two of the remaining three columns as well.

This was an early example of the newspaper custom of giving over the front page to advertisements. It was to be a long time before news was to return to it. Even the London *Times* did not do so until the issue of 3rd May 1966.

Mr Nettleton was aware of the sales impact of this prime space, and he lowered the standard of advertisements slightly to sell his own wares. He had, it appears a dab line in patent medicines. Readers were invited to obtain from him, by appointment at the *Royal Cornwall Gazette* Office, supplies of Barclay's original ointment and Dixon's anti-bilious pills.

Of Barclay's original ointment, he prints (2nd July 1814):

> *To Families and School* — It is a fact verified by daily experience, that the utmost care and attention are inadequate to prevent even the most respectable establishments from the attacks of that unpleasant and troublesome disorder, the ITCH ......

No less sweeping in its commendation is the claim for Dixon's pills. After asserting cures have been gratefully experienced by such aristocratic luminaries as the Duke of Bedford, the Dowager Lady Say and Sele, the Viscountess Bulkeley, Sir George Warren etc., etc., Mr Nettleton coaxes his readers with a description:

> The pills are found to be an incomparable remedy for restoring the tone of the stomach, for preventing crudities and their consequent disagreeable efluctations and flatulencies, sick head-ach [sic] and heartburn which is occasioned by pregnancy, and a debilitated stomach whether arising from the acrimony of the redundant bile or drinking to access.

To this colourful advice, the proprietor of the *Gazette*, purveyor of pills and ointments, too, adds his trump card. Yet another titled gentleman is a devotee, and a fulsome one at that:

> *From the Hon J. Massey*
> Sir, – I have found great benefit from Mr Dixon's Antibilious Pills, which I got at Oxford. I should thank you to send me two or three large boxes as soon as you can, to take with me into the country, being the only Family Medicine I am now in the habit of using.

In subsequent editions, Mr Nettleton showed himself equally concerned with the nation's health, increasing his scope by selling insurance and odd lots from time to time.

The paper, however, retained its standard and reputation throughout the fourteen years of Mr Nettleton's tenure. For a year after his death, his wife took over the paper.

With the issue of 27th June 1818 (No 783) there appeared the name of the new publisher and printer, F. Shoberl. His first front page reflects a respect for fair play that is not often found so free of reservation in the Press of today. Of the 6 columns, 4½ are classified advertisements, leaving only 1½ for news, but this half column is wholly taken up with a correction from H.H. Vivian, of Truro, relating to the report of a speech at the hustings in the previous week's issue. Magnanimous, one might agree, when it was Mr Nettleton to whom the letter must have been addressed.

Immediately following this election, there was a ball and supper given by the successful candidates at the Assembly Rooms. It was attended by what the reporter described as a 'select assemblage of the beauty and fashion in Truro and its vicinity'. He paid a fine tribute to Mr Pearce, the caterer who, 150 years ago, had a hard time compared to the caterer of any similar function today. This is what he wrote about the party:

> ... The supper provided by Mr Pearce surpassed in elegance every entertainment of the kind ever witnessed in Truro, and consisted of a profusion of delicacies procured for the occasion from Exeter as well as from different parts of this County. Considering the short notice given to Mr Pearce the arrangements reflected the highest credit on his diligence. At twelve [midnight] about 100 sat down to supper. Dancing recommenced at two with quadrilles led off by Lord F. Somerset and Miss James. The amusements of the evening terminated with Spanish dances, and the company did not cease to 'trip it on the light fantastic toe' till long after sunrise ....

As well as such pleasing items of leisure activity as the foregoing, the paper also brought news and views of many subjects from several Continents to the notice of its readers in the West Country; and these readers, probably included 'almost every gentleman (each) having a newspaper sent him by the post three times a week from London, when many gentlemen have even a daily paper sent them, and when each of them therefore feels his spirit, in Cornwall or Cumberland, as much alive as to national affairs, as if he lived in the bustle of the Strand or breathed the air of St. James's.'

The above quote comes from the *Gazette* of 1803 and refers to Cornish readers of London papers only, but between them and the time which we are now considering (1818), the paper produced some 7000 weekly issues and, as a well established paper certainly had a healthy circulation.

Apart from news despatches from abroad, there was also extensive coverage of 'Domestic Intelligence' from all over the country. Parliamentary news, London Stock Market, Corn Exchange, Smithfield and Leadenhall Markets were reported week by week. Mining news was to the forefront. Perhaps the most interesting items to the modern reader are those that have long since vanished into limbo: the Tallow market, the candles at Tallow Chandler's Hall, the Hemp (duty paid), the hay and straw. And surely the heart quickens when one reads the 'Falmouth Packet List'.

For example, the list on 1st August 1818 records the activities of the Post Office Packets to and from Falmouth for the preceding seven days, and consists of information under five headings. These are: Name of ship, name of captain, destination, and date of sailing. The fifth column is only partially filled as it records the arrivals during that week against their date of departure.

Above the columns is set out general information of the services under the heading, 'Order of sailing':

For *Lisbon* every Friday, from April to October, and Saturdays afterwards.
For *Barbadoes* and *Jamaica* and *America*, on the Sunday after the first Wednesday in every month.
Leeward Islands on the Sunday after the third Wednesday in every month.
Brazils, on the Saturday after the first Tuesday in every month.
The Packets for the Mediterranean sail every three weeks. — next sailing day on 14th August.

From the table that follows one gleans the fact that the round trip from Falmouth to America took about 90 days, to Brazils (sic) 135 days, Leeward Islands 95 days, Lisbon 30 days, Jamaica 105 days.

If one takes a random list in mid-winter, 28th February of the same year, 1818, one finds that the Brazils trip took 135 days, Lisbon 30 days, Jamaica 93 days, and Leeward Islands 90 days. There was no arrival from America that week, but three winter trips averaged 105 days.

Further shipping intelligence in each issue of the paper was contained in nearly two columns of the 'Coast List'. This consisted of movements during the preceding week in each of the following ports, in this order: Falmouth, Plymouth, Truro, Charlestown, Fowey, St Ives, Padstow, Hayle, Penzance, Scilly, Bristol.

Communications within the South-West were such that the

intelligence from Falmouth was predictably hot; from Plymouth 1 day late, Truro 1 day late, Charlestown 2 days, Fowey 2 days, Padstow 1 day, Hayle 1 day, Penzance 1 day and Scilly 2 days late.

The information provided was the name of the vessel, the surname of the Captain, and where she had come from or where she was bound. Some 400 movements were recorded each week.

Mr Shoberl continued the policy of encouraging readers to contribute to the correspondence columns. The phraseology and thinking displayed in these letters is often heavily sanctimonious. In the paper of 7th November 1818, there appears an example of ponderous give and take. In spite of no less than twelve columns of correspondence being taken up by mutual accusations over the business of United Mines, nevertheless, Mr Shoberl found space for the following:

> To the Editor of the *Cornwall Gazette*
> Truro, 4th November, 1818
> Sunday last, being on the 1st of November, the anniversary of electing a Mayor for the ensuing year for the borough of St Ives, the choice was prevented by the absence of a majority of the Corporation, who being otherwise engaged in the solemn duties of the day did not attend such public assembly, supposing that controversy might attend the determination. This so irritated the party assuming the claim to magisterial power (as they called it) that a want of propriety on their part produced such indecent expressions and conduct, intending thereby to reflect on the good order and respectable deportment of the then chief magistrate, that the most respectable part of the assemblage, disgusted at the abusive language then prevailing, retired with the Mayor to the Church, where, in attending divine service, they had the high gratification to hear proper hints given for the prevention of such indecent occurrences in future.
> I am Etc.
> A Stranger and Eye-Witness

To which, two weeks later, was printed the following reply:

> 1st November 1818

Sir,

I observed with some surprise in the *Cornwall Gazette* of last week, a letter from your Correspondent EUPHROSYNE in which she has remarked with much asperity on the admission of persons into the gallery of the Assembly-Room. I mean not to discuss the propriety or impropriety of such admission, but merely to state to your correspondent, who *professes* to be a stranger, that those whom she is pleased to designate as the commonality of the town, were some of the most respectable class of its inhabitants, that so far from annoying anyone by jeers or sarcasms, their demeanour was in the highest degree exemplary; and that their number (about 14) could not have contributed much to the heat of the room.

EUPHROSYNE may not, perhaps, be aware that a fee is levied at the entrance door, which effectually prevents the admission of improper persons. Had she taken the trouble to secure information on these points, she would not perhaps have so publicly expressed her sentiments on what might at first have appeared to her an impropriety; unless indeed *Alecto* be a more appropriate designation of her character than that of *Euphrosyne*.

J.W.

There is a report in the adjoining column of a lecture by Mr Potts to the Cornwall Literary and Philosophical Institution.

The subject of his lecture was the natural history of Cornwall, and, speaking on this November day, he remarked on the flowers and produce on display on the table before him. Everything, he said, had been grown in the open air of Cornwall, and among the exhibits were ripe strawberries and raspberries. Later on he referred to our now extinct Cornish Chough, remarking that he kept one of these birds in a domesticated state, which always greeted his friends with a soft engaging note, though with strangers he was both vociferous and pugnacious.

On 4th December 1819, the *Royal Cornwall Gazette* was bought by Thomas Richard Gillet, jun., and he was proprietor and publisher till his death in 1835, after which his father sadly assumed control 'for the exclusive benefit of the widow and three children'. For the following 28 issues the widow, Louisa Elizabeth Gillet, had her name shown as printer and publisher, but then Edward Wintour, of St Clement, took over.

A letter from a correspondent written shortly after Mrs Gillet assumed her place as a newspaper publisher shows that there were protesting conservationists then, as now, and that they, too, had the newspaper as their friend and forum for disseminating their views;

To the Editor

Redruth, 14th November 1835

Sir,
   Your correspondent in last week's paper describing himself a 'Cornishman' is, I conceive, justly entitled to the commendation of every lover of antiquity for his attempt to draw the attention of the Committee to the Dunstanville 'Testimonial to the preservation of the rock monuments on Carn Brea Hill.'

Living in the immediate vicinity of this castle-crowned Torr and *knowing* the veneration in which these remains of a remote and bye-gone age are held by all classes of the community nothing I am sure – not even the perpetuating by a column the rememberance of the late Lord de Dunstanville's virtues – will compensate in their esteem for the destruction or mutilation only, of these far-famed Druidical relics.

But, sir, sorry am I to inform you that the work of destruction has been going on for some time-past, a fact which from the long period which has elapsed since your correspondent visited the spot he appears not to have been acquainted with.

In Dr Borlase's time it had even been begun, for on page 119 of the *Antiquities* he says, 'great devastations have lately been made in the monuments of this remarkable hill by stone-cutters;' and within the last year or two the workmen employed by the Hayle Railway Company have made sad havoc among these granite heaps, and entirely disfigured the north-eastern face of the hill.

I sincerely hope therefore that all further depredations on the rock basins of Carn Brea will be entirely discounced by the subscribers to the erection of the proposed column, and

in whatever spot this edifice may be raised, I would use the language of a noble lord and exclaim,
------ let no busy hand
deface these scenes, already how defaced
I am, Sir, your obedient Servant,
ANTIQUARIUS

In September of 1836, a governmental decision of major importance to newspaper proprietors occurred. This was the reduction of the crippling Stamp Duty from 4d to a 1d. It had the effect of the *Gazette* reducing its price per copy with its issue No 1732 of 16th September to 4½d. It had been sold at 7d since 1815 when the tax was last increased.

This penal tax dated back to the end of the fifteenth century when Caxton set up his press in the precinct of Westminster Abbey. As already mentioned, from the very first the invention of printing was seen as a threat to the monopoly held by the ecclesiastics of the spread of knowledge. The Establishment, feeling the same foreboding as that which was to be shown by its successors toward education for the masses in the nineteenth century, saw to it through laws and taxation that the path of the printer would not be made easy. All too easily the spread of knowledge would become the spread of power.

Trevelyan, in his *English Social History* remarks:

> If Chaucer's spirit could have peeped over the shoulders of Edward VI at the machine which Master Caxton had brought from Flanders, as it stamped off in quick succession copies of the *Canterbury Tales* to look almost like real manuscripts, the flattered poet would have smiled at so pleasant a toy. He would hardly have foreseen it as a battering ram to bring abbeys and castles crashing to the ground, a tool that would ere long refashion the religion and commonwealth of England.

There remained yet a tax per copy of 1d until 1855, when this was abolished by the worthy Mr Gladstone, whereupon the static nature of newspaper development that had been in evidence for three centuries was assailed by a flood tide of activity from which, through the years that were to follow, only a minority were to survive for any length of time.

The tax burden on a newspaper largely explains the few

survivors, or even attempts at survivial, that were published before the mid-nineteenth century. Caxton came with his Press to England in 1476 yet the first English newspaper the *Weekly News* (Bourne and Archer) did not appear until 1622.

Prior to the abolition of the tax in 1855, an additional burden was imposed on a rural newspaper by the large size of its catchment area and the lack of easy communication. Four years later came the completion of the Royal Albert Bridge and the spread of a rail network in Cornwall. Though purely local newspapers did not have as much to gain, those newspapers printed in Plymouth and Truro that sought, and merited with their coverage of national news, circulation throughout Cornwall and the West Country were quick to take advantage of the new facilities.

And many a reporter must have felt it was about time, too. The best a *Gazette* reporter might have hoped for was for two rival papers to share a gig or chaise; or for him to have a ride on horseback perhaps fifteen or twenty miles through winter wind and rain after reporting a long meeting. On one occasion such a journey was described as 'somewhat wearisome'.

This restriction of facilities for both the collection of news and the distribution of a newspaper was another factor, of course, that slowed down all development. Indeed, between 1736 when the first newspaper began to circulate at all in Cornwall (the *Sherborne Mercury*) and the middle of the nineteenth century, there were only two papers printed in Cornwall that were able to survive. These were the *Royal Cornwall Gazette* and the *West Briton*.

Even at the time of the birth of the *Western Morning News* in 1860 no branch railways yet existed to take copies of papers swiftly to the rural areas of Cornwall; but communication between London and Plymouth was not at all bad, though there was only single line rail traffic to Plymouth from Exeter. The regular coach runs had by now been operating astonishingly reliably for a century. Their timetables were as follows: The journey from Devonport to London by the 'Quicksilver' took 21½ hours, allowing 10 minutes in Exeter and 13 minutes in Andover for meals. The journey demanded 21 changes of horses and was covered at an average of just on 11 miles an hour.

The shortest route between Exeter and Plymouth was a hilly one via Ashburton and was puncutally made every day in 4½ hours.

The 'Bath Mail' left Exeter at 5 in the evening reaching Plymouth at 10.30 p.m. Four hours for the journey was the normal, but three and a half hours was frequently achieved.

The 'Telegraph' stage coach was limited to 17 hours, day after day, between Exeter and London.

When the *Western Morning News* was launched, the railways still had the broad gauge, and it was to take twenty-five years before the whole line was converted to narrow gauge. Conditions were uncomfortable. From 1860 at least the carriages on the London train were covered, but there was no heating, no lavatories, and just one oil lamp swinging from the roof to serve two compartments. A ten minute stop was allowed at Swindon.

I may seem to have departed somewhat from the substance of Mr Flindell's creation, but communications are the arteries of a newspaper and these few examples I have mentioned surely are as interesting to us more than a century later as they would have been to him, when he started the paper more than half a century earlier.

Now then, on 1st June 1810, John Heard published from 30 Boscawen Street, Truro, the first edition of the new paper, the *West Briton*, the paper that had emerged from the liberal element of the population in opposition to Flindell and his *Royal Cornwall Gazette*. This first issue edited by Edward Budd, and type set and copies run off by hand, was of four pages, twenty-one by seventeen inches, and cost 6½d.

At once Flindell reacted with furious venom. Literally columns of indignation and criticism against the effrontery of the new paper were written by him over the following weeks and months, and it was not surprising that Budd was provoked into responding sometimes more intemperately than was his nature. Indeed, for three years, surely boring their readers, Flindell and Budd carried on this ferocious personal battle in their leaders. One example of this vituperous give and take is as follows:

When it was less than six months old the *West Briton* came out with a leader headed, 'The Infamous Falsehoods of the *Royal Cornwall Gazette* Exposed', and proceeded: 'Checked by no sense of shame, and influenced by no principle of honour, the scurrilous advocate on Ministerial imbecility vociferates falsehood after falsehood in order to drown the voice of truth.'

This was followed two months later by an open letter to Flindell from Budd:

Sir, – It is, I confess, with some reluctance that I prevail upon myself to address a man who has forfeited every claim to private trust or public confidence – yet as you are not too base to be employed by a certain faction, you are on this account entitled to some notice, though as an individual you are sunk below contempt.

This letter, hardly one to bring sunshine between Lemon and Boscawen Street, concluded, 'Surely if all sense of shame had not forsaken you, you would hide your head and shrink from observation.' The lusty child of liberalism already disdained respect for its elders.

Flindell left the *Gazette* in 1813 to take over the *Western Luminary* at Exeter, so that dust was allowed to settle in Truro. Later, some ten years later, he wrote a book emanating from his biblical studies and, with the intention, one can hopefully surmise, of being charitable, sent a copy to Budd in Truro. In doing this he intimated that he hoped soon to be visiting Truro, when he assured his old adversary it would not be his fault if they did not shake hands.

The obituary notice of Flindell that appeared in the *West Briton* two years later surely reveals that the feud had been de-fused. Certainly written by Budd it read:

Died. — On Sunday, at Exeter, after a protracted illness, Mr Thomas Flindell, Proprietor and Editor of the *Royal Cornwall Gazette*. As the conductor of a public journal, Mr Flindell's talents are well-known and fully appreciated in Cornwall, his native county. He possessed a vigorous mind, and a spirit which induced him to court rather than avoid situations of difficulty.

The violent political, and too often personal contest between Mr Flindell, as editor of the *Royal Cornwall Gazette*, and the editor of the *West Briton* which commenced on the establishment of the latter paper, and which was continued for several years, will not speedily be forgotten.

We owe it to Mr Flindell's memory to say that upwards of twelve months since, he made an amicable communication to his former opponent, stating that all feelings of personal hostility had ceased on his part and desiring a similar assurance in return. This overture was received as it ought to have been and replied to in corresponding spirit by the individual to whom it was addressed.

The leader writer of the *West Briton* fifty years later recalling this early period remarked:

> A tiny sheet it was which, in the summer of 1810, greeted the public eye. Yet with that little sheet great interests were identified. To estimate the influence of a local journal upon public opinion, it must be borne in mind that at that time very few London papers found their way into Cornwall. It was only in the houses of the wealthy, or at some of the principal hotels, that the *Morning Chronicle, Courier* or *Times* could be met with.
> The faint political illumination shed upon the Cornish mind was mainly through the columns of print originally established at Falmouth and afterwards transferred to Truro by Thomas Flindell, a man of sprightly and versatile mind, but an unscrupulous partisan of the Tory magnates who held the county politically as a private property.
> It was easy to cast the stigma of disaffection on those who encouraged a journal opposed to the ruling powers. This was a favourite mode of dealing with its supporters. The pettiest innkeeper, dribbling the squashiest beer from the roadside tap 10 miles from a market town, if he took the *West Briton* was suspected of being unfavourable to the government. Very timid people had it sent them under other people's addresses. The articles and news it contained were read by many by stealth, as if they were contraband.
> A journal which ventured to deny the independence of the electors of Grampound and St Mawes, or the purity even of Truro . . . . . . would naturally attract to itself a great deal of ill feeling and party spite.
> But the man who does no harm to himself can rarely be harmed much by others. Mr Budd, the editor, went calmly on, through good report and evil report, and lived to see the principles he advocated become those of the great mass of his countrymen. Without any undue assumption we may award to him the credit of having kindled much of the liberal and

patriotic feeling by which Cornwall has since been so honorably disinguished.

Though the paper was given a good start on its still flourishing career by Budd; it has also owed much to other figures, to the Heards, to Latimer, to Redding in its creation, to Joseph Thomas and William Hooper and Henry James and T.E. Williams, and to the Heards again, all men who met the conflicts and contrasts of the industrial revolution with prescience and equanimity from the hot seat of the editorial chair.

Yet it is to an editor who assumed this chair as recently as 1947 that the *West Briton* owes a special dept, for shortly before he died, he completed a definitive history of the paper, now difficult to come by, entitled *From Stage Coach Days to the Jet Age— The Story of the West Briton in Nine Reigns*. It is to him that the reader of this piece on the *West Briton* owes recognition for its authenticity and interest. Claude Berry died when yet quite young, but he leaves Cornwall the richer for the clarity of his writing and his taste for its history, works that stand on our library shelves for our study and enjoyment, and for the enrichment of all who care for Cornwall.

In common with its rival in Truro, the *West Briton* found it difficult from the first to overcome the fiscal charges that dug deep into revenue. Not only in the early days was the stamp duty 3½d per copy, increasing to 4d in 1814, but a surcharge of three shillings and sixpence was made on each advertisement whether it was for a servant girl seeking a place, or a landowner selling an estate. There was, however, a curious dispensation regarding the stamp duty. A paper was allowed to be sent free for fourteen days following publication.

I have mentioned earlier the stigma attached to a reader of the new liberal paper in many quarters, so that 'the articles and news it contained were read by many by stealth, as if they were contraband'. Nowadays it is inconceivable that could ever have been the case in Cornwall, but the *West Briton* had been founded for a political purpose and it pulled no punches in its fight for the ends its founders desired the nation to achieve. This was Parliamentary reform, with the abolition of the 'rotten boroughs', Catholic emancipation and the reduction of taxation.

Not all innkeepers were deterred from taking the *West Briton* because of its liberal policy and the fierce attacks made upon it. Less than two months after its publication the front page carried a 'Notice to the Public' emanating from the inn which gave the village of Indian Queens its name. The notice ran:

> Whereas some ill-disposed person or persons have propagated a report that Mr Symonds, of the Indian Queen, did express himself in a very improper and disrespectful manner respecting the gentlemen who support the *West Briton* and that he refused to allow the said paper to be left at his house for any persons in his neighbourhood who might wish to take it, Mr Symonds feels it necessary to declare that such reports are wholly unfounded; that he takes in the *West Briton* for the accommodation of his customers, and that he has no objection to allowing the paper to be left at his house for any persons who may desire it. Mr Symonds begs to observe that he does not in any wise interfere with political controversy, judging it to be his duty to accommodate and endeavour to give satisfaction to the Nobility, Gentry, etc., who may favour his house.

Claude Berry takes up the story of the paper's growth, reaching up to the triumph of the policy it advocated being enshrined in the passing of the Great Reform Bill.

> It had passed through the House of Commons in 1831 but had been thrown out by the House of Lords, and the *West Briton* of 14th October 1831 appeared in deep mourning with a heavy border of black on its front and back pages. But the victory was just around the corner. In the following year the Reform Bill passed into law.
> The first election under the Municipal Reform Act took place on 26th December, 1835, and resulted in a resounding victory for the Reform candidates. Budd, the editor of the paper and by that time a part proprietor of it, did not live to celebrate the triumph, for a grave illness, which had failed either to subdue or silence his powerful advocacy ended fatally just before the election results became known.

Three weeks after his death, on 13th June, 1823, the name Elizabeth Heard appeared in the imprint as printer and publisher. She was the widow of John Heard, who had been in at the beginning as proprietor and who had died twelve years before at the age of forty-two. She proved to be a remarkably able woman much admired for her business acumen and consideration. Only thirty-five when she took over she was 'to remain in charge for forty-four years. Berry writes, 'Over "a dish of tea" in her pleasant parlour above the stationer's and booksellers' shop in Boscawen Street, Cornish writers, established and aspiring, often came to talk to their friend and confidante.'

The new editor was Joseph Thomas, a Wesleyan minister from Cheshire, and he was fortunate in the staff he had around him. At their head, as chief reporter, was Isaac Latimer, a brilliant young Londoner who began work as a stenographer, and who, soon after Queen Victoria's accession, came to Truro. He was the first shorthand writer to practise his craft west of the Tamer. Ten years later he moved to Plymouth to edit the *Plymouth Journal*.

I shall now leave it to Claude Berry to speak for himself on the next stage in the paper's growth under one of the most revered characters in the paper's history, Edward Goodridge Heard, son of John and Elizabeth.

> This eighteen-year-old was learning the trade in all its branches, and must have profited greatly from Latimer's experience and ability. Until the railway era had opened in Cornwall, news-gathering in the County was a slow and difficult business. Young Heard developed into an ardent news-gatherer, and continued so after he had engaged in heavy managerial work.
>
> Long before her death in 1867, in her 84th year, his versatile and gifted mother must have felt confident that the future of the *West Briton* would be assured in the keeping of her son. By 1867 the paper had greatly expanded. The expansion had begun in 1851 when the size was increased from four pages to eight. To celebrate the paper's Jubilee in 1860, new and improved type was used and this enabled four further columns to be added.
>
> But the main feature of the Jubilee number was that for the

first time the paper was printed on a flat-bed press operated by steam power. Thence forward, though the paper continued to publish national and foreign news, much more space was devoted to Cornish news, and especially that relating to Cornish mining and agriculture. It was one of E.G. Heard's outstanding contributions to the paper that he concentrated so much attention to the county's mining industry both as a newspaper man and as a discriminating 'adventurer', the term by which investors were known. 'In bright days and in dark', wrote the leader writer of the *Western Morning News* shortly after his death, in 1899, 'he was a mainstay of the Cornish mining industry.'

This is not the place to consider the *West Briton's* fortunes in the present century, but one is happy to record an event of surely emotional significance, namely, the union of the *West Briton* and its old rival the *Royal Cornwall Gazette*, exactly 150 years after Flindell had laid its foundations in Falmouth. As the latter name is included in the title of the *West Briton* today, thus, today, the Three Graces still provide the news for Cornish readers whose forbears knew them all those years ago. Just look at this extraordinary record of service by these news dispensers to our fortunate County: the *Royal Cornwall Gazette* – 150 years, the *Western Morning News* (yes, let's bring that in) – 116 years, the *West Briton* – 167 years.

How pale today looks all the feudin' and fussin' between Mr Flindell and Mr Heard all those years ago. And how delightful to be able to bid them a happy farewell on this note of gratitude for splendid service.

V

The Young Tangye Brothers of Illogan

The inlet of Porth Bay, just north of Newquay, is just beginning to open to us. One arm of this long, rather than broad, inlet, the northern one, includes the ancient cliff castle of Trevelgue Island, its bulk jutting out along the length of it and out to sea. From *Spray* it is looking like a massive dog asleep, with paws outstretched, and shoulders hunched.

Across the inlet on the other side, some three hundred yards only, are the open grounds of Glendorgal, its array of fine granite chimneys just visible above the tamarisk.

From the foregoing title to this piece you would be forgiven if you sensed a trace of nepotism in the air, and you would be right, for this is my home ground and I cannot pass by without paying tribute to my forbears, those five young men from the village of Illogan near Redruth. I hope I am not mistaken in thinking their story of how they made a name for themselves will interest all those whom I seek to please.

It will serve my inclination if I were to drop *Spray's* anchor here in the home waters of Newquay Bay, but past experience tells me I would not spend an altogether tranquil night. Anchoring off a lee shore is not wholly comfortable at the best of times, for a change in the wind while you are asleep can, at the best cause you to up anchor and away; and, at the worst, drive you shoreward onto beach or rock.

The degree of probability may be low, but the ghosts of all the vessels lying wrecked at the foot of the cliffs we have sailed past prove that when wind and sea and sailor are in conflict, the sailor's skill is not always enough to quell the effect of the storm.

My training leads me to look ahead. *Spray* and I are making for Falmouth. Our mooring is in the gentle river Fal, opposite Malpas.

The Young Tangye Brothers of Illogan 101

To get there we must pass 'round the corner', round Land's End. The ever wild and dramatic coastline yields us no shelter. From Newquay southward, I see feathery clouds forming high up against fading blue sky, and the wind is slightly stronger than it has been and has backed a point. There's still five hours sailing before we reach the Longships, and I will prefer to be round the corner rather than have the north coast to leeward.

So I shall not drop anchor here, but take my time, enjoy a cup of coffee, and pause to think awhile of my grandfather, Richard and his family, as they were a century and a half ago.

But, at first, I find it hard to free my mind from the fate on that terrible winter's day of the *Hodbarrow Miner*, hurled onto the shore at Mawgan Porth. And how, on that same day, young Storey of the Newquay lifeboat, *James Stephens 5*, was washed overboard and drowned, just where *Spray* and I so peacefully ride now. May the souls of the wrecked rest in peace.

On 3rd November 1856 there was a great concourse of people assembled at the Thames-side shipyard of Napier and Son on the Isle of Dogs. They were there to watch the launching of an iron steamship larger by far then any yet built, and not to be surpassed in size until the *Mauretania* fifty years later.

Little wonder that the ship's immensity, conceived and created by that great engineer, Isambard Brunel, had attracted the attention of shipping interests all over the world, spilling over into public consciousness that it was a spectacular marvel, symbolic of the rising industrial might of the new Victorian age.

So it was that on the day, the 3,000 spectators who crowded into the Yard to watch the launch were at a pitch of excitement that was heightened by that psychic thrill of awareness that they were at the focus of a great event.

The moment they awaited at last arrived. There was an overwhelming hush, then the thud of the hammers driving away the wedges holding back the cradles ...... She moved a foot, two feet. The crowd roared, 'She moves! she moves!' And then she stopped. The cheering continued, then slackened, then dwindled into silence. Full power was applied to the steam rams designed to shift her great mass down the slipway. But she was not going to move any further.

No, she wouldn't budge! Nothing could shift her. Horror! Appalling embarrassment all round to say the very least.

For the following three months the great ship clung to the stocks while the whole engineering establishment were at a loss to know what to do.

The *Leviathan* (for this was her name, later the *Great Eastern*) remained stonily stubborn, resisting, quietly but purposefully, or so it seemed, the combined experience of the greatest engineers, here and abroad, here and across the seas.

However, four unknown young Cornishmen, brothers from the village of Illogan, came to the unlikely rescue. They got the great ship moving into the water, this huge vessel that would not move for anybody else. The fifth brother came later.

It is these young men to whom I now propose to introduce my reader.

Broad Lane is a minor road connecting the Redruth/Camborne highway with Illogan. About half a mile along Broad Lane, on the left, is a small single-storey building set back a few yards from the road. It has a door flanked by a window either side. It is the village hall and, on a rough stone slab above the door, is carved the legend, undated, 'To the Memory of the Tangye family'.

Leaving aside its innocent assumption that I and the rest of the current generation of Tangyes are no longer around, it is a touching tribute to the truly astonishing family that was brought up in the first half of the last century in the small dwelling, still standing and occupied, a few yards along the other side of the road.

From this family of nine children, five brothers were destined to create, while still young men in their twenties and thirties, an engineering business whose name was known around the world. The firm, Tangye's Ltd, of Cornwall Works, Solihull Birmingham, was soon going to employ 5,000 men, and to pioneer many industrial social services, including the five and a half day week and nine-hour day. I quote from the *Yorkshire Post*, at the time of Richard Tangye's death in 1906, in which readers were reminded that he and the brothers and the firm had given a quarter of a million sterling for educational, religious, artistic and philanthropic services to the town of Birmingham.

That is a measure of the achievement of these boys from Broad Lane; so why should they have been able to do it? Who were their parents? What was their upbringing? Before I unfold their story before you I would like to bring your attention to coincidences which befell me while researching.

The hunt by the researcher for his prey can be long and tedious, but it is enlivened by the ever-present prospect of an unexpected revelation, and rewarded by the capture from the past of yet another truth.

Yet in one's enthusiasm for learning more about the past one must be careful. It was not long ago that Sir Hugh Casson said, 'Guard against worship for its own sake ... the danger is that we can become a nation of museum keepers showing the church and the old manor house at 20 pence a time.'

However, I have no doubt my readers can, with impunity, enjoy evidence of the merging of life between generations, the continuing relationship between the living and the dead.

One of Hamilton Jenkin's many fascinating books is called *News from Cornwall*. It relates to one William Jenkin, who was steward of the Lanhydrock Estate at the end of the eighteenth and beginning of the nineteenth centuries. The book is largely in the form of letters in relation to this stewardship (1792-1820).

The letters reveal the delightful character of William and the fascinating details of Cornish life from that of gentry to miners. The book impressed itself on my mind and imagination to an extraordinary degree though, to my knowledge, I had no cause to have any personal interest.

I came to like William Jenkin immensely, so that when Alfred his son became an assistant in the office of this prestigious estate I shared his father's delight — and it was not long before one realised that William was proudly looking to Alfred to step into his shoes on retirement.

Few plans turn out neatly, however and I found very touching William's concern for his son and the worry he felt; for Alfred was not particularly bright, and perhaps would not prove himself suitable to take his place as steward to the family he served and loved.

William's concern for Alfred was such that he found himself having to take on extra duties at an advanced age hoping it would lead to openings for his son. The book ends with the death of William in his home, Trewirgie, in 1820, aged eighty-two.

Now it so happened that shortly after I had finished this book, I found a small volume of reminiscences privately published in 1904 by George Tangye, one of the five brothers. With my mind still filled with echoes from William Jenkin's life I read now, to my astonishment, that George's younger brother, John, had worked for *five years*, 'at Redruth in the Estate Office of *Alfred* Jenkin, who was chief steward to Mr Robarts'. I was delighted. So Alfred *did* get the job after all.

John Tangye, however, died at the age of twenty. But it transpired that this was the occasion for another link to be forged with the Jenkin family, for it was none other than George who took his brother's place for the following year.

And now the postscript. Interested in the life of my great-grandfather, Joseph, father of the family in Broad Lane, and of whom I will be speaking later on, I had learned that he was a Quaker, and that he and the family attended the Friends Meeting House in Redruth to which, every Sunday, they walked in pairs, one behind the other, and dressed in their Quaker habit.

When Joseph died, aged fifty-seven in 1852, it was here that he was buried, so one day I went to see if I could find his grave. I was not expecting the wholly satisfying experience that awaited me that afternoon.

The Meeting House, and its pretty garden and cemetery, is secluded, and surrounded by a high wall with tall trees outside its boundaries shielding it from the winds and elements. From the path encircling the little building I stepped into the smooth green sward of the cemetery and turned to read the words on the face of the first two tombstones that faced me. I bent down to read the inscriptions. I was standing at the graves, side by side, of Joseph and Anne, my great-grandfather and great-grandmother!

I had not been prepared to find their graves – at any rate, not so easily – and the sudden reality of Joseph and Anne, of whom I had read so much, lying so close to me now, was curiously exhilarating. I had a feeling of security come over me, a realisation of the continuity of human existence be it temporal or spiritual.

But then, as I turned away, my eye caught the name on the very next stone. It was Jenkin. To my disbelief it was none other than the same William Jenkin of Lanhydrock. And then, next to him, a yard further on lay amazingly, but somehow I felt inevitably, dear Alfred.

I find it uncanny that I had been so taken with, so wrapped up in their lives, thanks to Hamilton Jenkin's sensitive book, while being totally unaware of their connection with the Tangyes of Broad Lane in life, and now in death.

Some years later I got a clue how it came about. It was the Tangyes' landlord who must have effected the introduction of John to the Estate Office, for the freehold of the land on which stood the Broad Lane cottage and holding was none other than Mrs Agar of Lanhydrock.

An attempt to visualise the life of the family when the children were still at home – from the mid-1820's to the end of the forties – is stimulated by the fact that so little has changed, visually speaking.

There remains a commanding symbol linking yesterday with today, for if you stand at the door of the cottage and look down the road to the south, the dominating view of Carn Brea silhouetted against the sky-line has not changed at all; and atop it is the tall, massive Bassett column, there since 1836.

This time-worn edifice tells its own tale, bears the strength of youth. Surely such survivors of man's craft and skill provide a most severe lesson to his pride, that his own works should thus outlive him, that generation after generation should live and die watched by the very buildings they themselves created.

It was from this timeless scene that emerged the four brothers who were to complement each other's genius. The fifth, Edward, played a less prominent part, emigrating to America at an early age, and re-joining the brothers later.

The organiser of the commercial side of the business, its inspiration, was Richard, the youngest but one; and the manager was George, while James, the eldest, was the innovator, inventor and craftsman, and Joseph, master craftsman and perfect junior partner to his elder brother.

Their father was a Joseph, too, and though he was a man with no particular mechanical bent, was working as a miner, I find, in the great Dolcoath mine in 1811.

The man who inspired the family interest toward engineering was Joseph's father-in-law, Edward Bullock (1776-1870) who, owing nothing to the gifts of fortune, and brought up on a farm in St Columb, had his own smithy, and later was in charge of the largest of the three Watt engines at Wheal Tolgus mine (86-inch). He was, in fact, a born mechanic with whom the boys spent much time.

At the same time Edward Bullock worked a holding of eight acres of land some of which was the other side of the road to the Broad Lane cottage, and through which the Portreath branch of the Hayle/Redruth railway ran. Opened in 1838, this was one of the first professionally managed public railway lines in Cornwall. It brought coal from Portreath to Redruth and Scorrier in one direction and in the other, ore to be smelted in Wales. This line served the Camborne/Illogan area of mines for thirty years.

Incidentally, the track is plainly visible today, and I was surprised to find that it ran along a quite massive embankment, which must have been a frustrating obstacle so far as the cultivation of the holding was concerned. It is still just as it was.

Edward Bullock had a plot of seven to eight acres here. He also leased another eight acres for which Joseph Tangye, his son-in-law, was sub-tenant. This plot is situated a few hundred yards from his cottage, in the crook caused by the join of Broad Lane and the Camborne/Redruth highway. It is now almost completely built over.

Edward Bullock was a tall, active man of over six foot. Right up to the last (he died aged ninety-five), he was nimble and energetic. He worked at Tolgus by night, and on his holding by day. Fortunately, the mine was only a half mile or so away, but his was a seventeen hour working day, and the rest he thought was seven hours wasted in sleep. In his 'spare time' he made fuses for the miners.

Of course, this was Trevithick country, Murdock country, a leading area in the kingdom for industry, so that it is not surprising that, with a dexterous smithy as a grandfather, who also managed a mine engine, and local talk being as much about engines and steam and mining as agriculture, any inherent interest in a child in engineering was free to blossom.

And the children of this family were fortunate in having

parents to whom tributes have been left by their sons which show how lucky they were.

George Tangye, in his little book privately printed in 1904 called *A Family Cruise*, wrote of them:

> My parents, Joseph and Anne Tangye (members of the Society of Friends) were peace-loving souls who pursued the even tenor of their way through life, the friends of everybody, and everybody their friend. My father, who was also a small coal merchant, kept the modest store, or village shop, where everything was sold which could be wanted by the country round – drapery, groceries, crockery and general haberdashery, and also a little stock of homely medicines.

Let me summarise the size of the family that lived in this small dwelling at Broad Lane:

There was James, Joseph, John, Edward, Richard and George; Anne, Alice and Sarah; and somewhere there was room for parents, too.

The children's ages spanned a period of twenty years. The two eldest were off to work probably at the age of twelve. James, soon to be the consummate technician and inventor around whose skills the works in Birmingham was to be begun, was placed, much against his will, with a local wheelwright. Joseph, the second son, was bound for a term to a shoeing smith. Both these positions held prestige, craftsmen such as smithy, wheelwright or carpenter having the distinction of not suffering the labourer's dependence on day to day work.

Richard, many years later, wrote of this time:

> While my brothers were engaged in their uncongenial occupations with the wheelwright and shoeing-smith they spent their evenings in a workshop at home, where they made working models of engines and other machines, while the younger ones turned the wheel of the lathe.
>
> My father was unable to see that any practical advantage was likely to accrue from this occupation, and often used to lament the waste of candles; but my mother, with a keener perception, recognised the natural bent of her sons' minds and encouraged its development. Unhappily, neither of

them lived to witness the ultimate results of her foresight. But it was not long before the brothers demonstrated that the candles were not wasted, for a little beam-engine which they made was sold for a sum that much more than paid for all the candles that they had used.

I am always fascinated when I have the opportunity to read someone's diary written long ago. The leap over the grave of a diarist's thoughts from then to the immediacy of the present, the banishment of time between conception and their kindling in my mind the original sense and feeling of the writer. This is surely a rare privilege to experience, one that permits intimacy between two people to an extent which might never exist were they even close friends at the time of pen being put to paper. So let me now quote from Anne Tangye's journal and listen to her speaking. She starts with a statement of explanation, added later:

> *1st January, 1837.* I was admitted a member into the Society of Friends, and my dear husband the year following.
> O, with how many mercies have our lives been crowned. O, may we hold fast the faith, and may our dear children with my dear parents, together with all that the arms of love can encompass, be favored in the enjoyment of the like precious faith.
> *April 4th, 1838:* Samuel and Sarah Rundell visited our meetings at Redruth/Camborne with much acceptance. What a prophet of the Lord is that man!
> *June 5th.* Dear Richard Bool visited us very much to my benefit and the unity that was amongst us, although I was very poor and solitary and full of weeping.
> *June 11th:* Mary Ann Keisl, a young woman, one of our neighbours, was crushed to death by the steam carriage.
> *July 12th:* Blessed Lord, what more is there in thy blessed will for me to suffer, it seems as if the deeps would swallow me up. I may say all thy billows have gone over me.
> *Dec. 26th:* Was at the Truro Quarterly Meeting wherein many living testimonies were borne that tended greatly through the Divine blessing to my strength and comfort for which I desire to praise God, for all his mercies.

But this comfort was not to last long. Within a few weeks, the family was to be sorely tried, but, with the blessed gift of faith that God had bestowed on her, she was prepared to accept God's will unreservedly.

On 1st February 1834 she wrote:

> Our dear children, Richard and George, are sorely afflicted with the measles, little hopes of their recovery. Richard has had an inflammation of the chest and is extremely ill in the night, the difficulty of breathing very great. George's fever is so violent that we fear he cannot hold it long. Dear children, what will we do? It seems resignation is called for. It brings to my remembrance blessed Abraham's case in his beloved Isaac, how gently he led him along toward the place of offering. Oh the precious sacrifice! Did Abraham look on his dear son and relent, or was his eye singly directed toward the father of all his mercies; to that God who gave, and in whose power alone it was to take away. May I like Abraham, have the strength to give back to God what he so kindly gave to me.

One can imagine Anne writing this by candlelight in the room, flickering shadows on the wall, with the two children fighting for breath, noisily striving for air, helpless and too young to share their mother's faith. But God had heard her, and two days later she writes, 'Today our dear children are both recovered which calls for fresh gratitude, thanksgiving and praise.'

On 18th December 1840: 'After a long and tedious confinement I was with great difficulty and danger, delivered of a child, who was a fine boy but died about the time of birth which seemed to us a source of great grief.'

Further sad entries are interspersed with beautiful simple passages relating to her faith. Her grandmother, Edmund Bullock's wife, died, and Sister Eleanor Caroline's 'dear little boy died ten days after he was scalded with boiling pease and was interred in the Friends' burying ground, Redruth' — the same where I was to find Anne and Joseph and John and Alfred Jenkin over a century later.

Death was a much more familiar visitor in a household than now, of course, but always, or nearly always, he brought with him sorrow and loss and the hopeless cry of the bereaved of what might have been, especially when the young were the object of his stealthy call. Reading this diary we can see the power of faith in combating the worst of his damage. Today faith is directed towards anti-biotics provided by the Health Service. How much better for a family to be bathed in the light of God with a faith which permeates everyday life and is not confined to the plea of the afflicted only when trouble looms, or as an excuse for secular celebrations at Christmas and Easter.

There is no doubt that the success of the Tangye industrial influence in the years to come, when the brothers were responsible for touching the lives of so many, that the example of their parents, Anne and Joseph, provided the heart of their concern for their neighbour.

In this diary there is much more that I would wish to tell you, but let me close it with the account she gives of the death of John, the brother who died at the age of twenty and of whom both George and Richard later wrote, 'John . . . he was the best of us!'

Anne wrote on 20th December 1847:

Our dear John Tangye was on his way to work at the office (Lanhydrock Estate office at Redruth) when he was taken bringing up blood and was obliged to return. The first week or two of his confinement some hopes entertained of his recovery, when he began to sink very fast, until on February 7th, when he ceased at once to work and live.

Very soon after his being taken ill he patiently submitted himself into the hands of his heavenly Father, saying that he knew it was in faithfulness that he was afflicted, and said, 'Not my will but thine, O Lord, be done'. He many times felt deep sorrow for sin, evident proof of repentance until at last he seemed to believe that the Lord had in much mercy freely forgiven him for all his sins. He said many things respecting the hope he had of his well-being in the happy world above which I fully believe was the case for he was favoured to enjoy sweet peace, his own will, I believe, being quite lost in that of his Heavenly Father.

John gave us many precious exhortations to prepare to meet him in heaven, which I humbly hope will be the case with every one of us, the earnest desire and prayer of his poor afflicted mother.

Towards the end of his life, George wrote of his mother thus:

> My mother. Words fail me here. No woman gave up her whole life more for her family and for those around her, and no mother more fully deserved the whole heart-and-soul devotion of her family than she did; and it was lovingly rendered to her.
>
> During an epidemic of the dread cholera, when no one else could be found to minister to the patient, she gratuitously took the duties upon herself and successfully nursed him through the attack.
>
> She was a very pretty woman, and as able as she was pretty, and a model of thriftiness. Among her sterling qualities was the happy gift of cheerfulness, and she knew how to keep her troubles to herself. She was my father's right hand, and more – for she managed the business and kept the accounts.
>
> Many of the poor miners could only pay when they received their wages, which was only once a month, but none of the dear old customers were sent away empty. My parents often came between them and the workhouse, and when pay-day came, they did the best they could.
>
> On Sunday mornings, the family attended the Friends Meeting two miles away. Everyone went, the youngest two-and-two, hand-in-hand, with father and mother coming last. We were all dressed in the primitive Quaker fashion, all 'spick-and-span'. And weren't we proud of mother! No one looked so nice, no one showed greater taste in her go-to-meeting dress than she did.

Illogan, at this time, had a population of over 9,000 which was only 2,000 less than Camborne and as much as 6,000 more that Truro. I do not know how many of the inhabitants were Church of England, but more were Dissenters; there was only one family of Quakers – the Tangyes.

The parson's duties, with few C. of E. parishioners, were therefore light, which should not have made any difference, one way or the other; but there was the Church Rate, and the law as to Tithes, and the parson, in that context, very much resented the smallness of his own flock, and took it out of those who disdained his ministrations. And he did this, quite legally, by collecting his dues from any and everyone, of his church or not of his church.

Joseph Tangye was generous and open-handed, of the same mould as his wife Anne. He was a man of unblemished character, but being a Quaker he was, as Richard, his son, has put it, 'a fly in the ointment which troubled the Christian spirit of the parson, living in his fine house in beautiful grounds.' To the poor, hardworking family in Broad Lane he would send, twice a year, officers of the law to distrain for the tithes and Church rates, at one time among other things seizing the cow upon which they depended.

These distraints were always made in the most aggravating fashion, every device for running up a long bill being resorted to, and seizing goods of a value greatly exceeding the value of the demand. Sometimes the distraints were made under circumstances of great brutality, and their parents had real difficulty in stopping the children taking the law into their own hands.

On one occasion, in particular, their anger was raised to white heat. Their mother was skilful, as was often the custom, at many domestic and culinary tasks, not least in bacon curing, and every autumn she would put aside a supply for the use of her family. Her skill reached the ears of the parson, and he sent the officers to make the annual distraint. Seizing it from the store they took it away for public auction. Let me quote now a reliable witness of the incident, one of the children:

> The parson could not, for decency's sake, to say nothing of it being against the law, bid in person at the sale; and as the public sympathised with us in our trouble, they misguidedly refrained from bidding. Consequently the parson got his bacon very cheaply.
>
> This was bad enough, but worse remained to come. A few days after the distraint, the parson's servant saw my mother and told her his master bade him say that 'the bacon was excellent, he had never tasted better in his life!

This experience of social injustice which included others such as the 'three lives' land tenure system, had a lasting effect on Richard. From it one can trace the conception of the advanced form of management/worker relationship he introduced at an early stage into the Cornwall Works; also, perhaps, his philanthropy, always unobtrusive except when alien forces and situations exposed the source.

Provided depredations by the occupant of the Illogan parsonage on cottage food stores allowed it, the forties were a comparatively prosperous time for the neighbourhood, although an anxiety was in the air which proved to be not displaced.

Fish was more or less the staple food of the poor and was abundant and brought fresh from the boat every day by what George describes as 'quick-running horses and carts'. Occasionally, the family was able to buy a cart load of pilchards from St Ives for twelve shillings.

A favourite breakfast dish through the winter were these salt-cured fish. Potatoes were always abundant everywhere, and that situation prevailed until the railway arrived in 1859, when the produce was taken away to London and elsewhere. How little times have changed today, when my fishmonger in Newquay has to buy fish from Hull.

I have referred to the life-long disgust that the bullying parson's exaction of his tithes had on Richard. Its memory was such that in his notable book on Cromwell, *The Two Protectors*, published in London in 1899, Richard uses his experience of this brutal aspect of the Established Church in his argument in favour of Cromwell.

Richard and George were together at the British School in Illogan in which there was one master and sixty pupils. The school took fee-paying pupils who got priority, so that the Tangye pupils got little attention. However, they made the most of it and the master earned their respect appointing Richard a monitor at eight years old, he having passed the test of being able to spell a five-syllabled word promptly and correctly.

It was here that on rare occasions the parson came to examine the pupils in their Scripture. On one of these visits George unconsciously gave him a rebuff which perhaps he did, or did not, appreciate.

The question he asked George was, 'Who is my neighbour?' George could not immediately reply, so the reverend gentleman said, 'Am I your neighbour?', and this time the reply was clear and precise. With unconscious vehemence George said, 'No! You're not!'

It was here that, when only nine years old, Richard fell during a boisterous game in the yard, and broke his arm. Some difficulty ensued over repairing the damage, and in due course it was realised he would never be able to use it for any manual labour. Living in an environment of machines and engineers — his grandfather, his two older brothers, and the elite of the community in Redruth and Camborne and Illogan — this was a tremendous blow. There had been only one future imaginable for the boys in the family, and that was to be artisans in this growth industry of the time, engineering.

When a catastrophe strikes, we are likely to say, with deep feeling, perhaps, 'Why has this happened to me? What have I done to deserve it?' Anne was one of those who, with faith in God, would weep, certainly, but she would have trust in His purpose and accept it was His will. When time passes and we look back at this or that catastrophe, sometimes its purpose becomes entirely clear, for if it had not happened, we discover that the jolt of it turned us on to a new road we would never have found without it. And further, we can see that it is the *right* road. To people like Anne, she sees her faith fulfilled and thanks God. To others the connection between cause and effect is allowed to pass by unnoticed, and the will of God never credited. How blind they are.

This accident to Richard proved to be a crucial point in his life, the jolt that was to put him on the road to fulfilment. When the doctor announced to his mother he had sustained a compound fracture which would always handicap him, he went on to remark that the boy had a good-sized head, so why not try what a little extra schooling would do for him?

The verdict was a calamity to the whole household, but soon the doctor's suggestion was taken seriously. The two elder brothers, James (ten years older than Richard) and Joseph were by this time beginning to earn their living, so extra schooling for Richard was not so far out of reach; and, indeed, he attended for the next three years the school in Redruth run by William Bellows.

George was also to become a pupil at this school, so at this time there emerged the pattern that was to form the structure of one of the greatest engineering firms of the 19th century, Tangye's Ltd., of Cornwall Works, Birmingham — James and Joseph the craftsmen and inventors, Richard and George the organisers.

While at Redruth Richard attended his first public meeting. Hitherto, his only experience of it was at the Friends Meeting House. But this occasion was to have a lasting influence on his life.

He was taken to hear a speech on a subject that could hardly have excited him. It was on 'Ocean Penny Postage', and the speaker was a man of such eloquence that the wealth of imagery he invoked before his audience was a revelation to the boy. His name was Elihu Burritt, and Richard referred to him as 'The learned American blacksmith'. In recalling the event, Richard wrote:

> His fine eyes kindled, as he appealed to the miners present to assist him in his self-imposed efforts to enable them to communicate easily and inexpensively with their relatives in the mines on Lake Superior. He pointed out it was not distance, but the costliness of communication, which caused alienation between members of families separated by stern necessity in their efforts to obtain a livelihood.
> And finally he showed that brotherhood between nations was best promoted by increasing the means of communication between them.

Perhaps this, too, shaped his later priority that he gave to keeping in contact with the agents of his company placed world-wide. Before the end of the century he had sailed round the world seven times, an achievement that today most of us would recognise as being something even by air.

Years afterwards, when Elihu Burritt was United States Consul in Birmingham, Richard called on him and told him how his oratory had inspired him nearly thirty years before.

At the age of thirteen Richard left the school in Redruth and, with the aid of the Society of Friends was sent to their school at Sidcot in Somersetshire. For a small boy the parting from Illogan must have been traumatic for all concerned because it would be a year before he came home again.

The journey to Sidcot was made by steamer from Hayle to Bristol and took about sixteen hours. A friend was waiting at Cumberland Dock to take him to school, which he found to be a 'truly admirable institution, feeling myself to be in an entirely new world and receiving thoroughly good training.'

At the end of the first year, the question of his future occupation had to be decided. Even then he instinctively felt a commercial life would suit him best, but he was dissuaded by sombre argument about its hazards, and reluctantly yielded to the suggestion by his tutor that he should become a pupil-teacher at the School — and so he was bound there until he would be twenty-one.

From the very first he felt unfitted for the work, and time did nothing to change things.

His duties were arduous. His day started at 5.30 in the morning and continued with little rest until 9 p.m., when the same bell that summoned the senior teachers to supper was his signal for bed. Even then his duties did not cease, for he was still responsible for good order in the bedrooms.

His work was performed under what he called 'very disagreeable conditions, known only to junior teachers in large schools who alone can tell how unhappy boys can make teachers who are only a little older than themselves.' On the other hand he did appreciate being able to use a good library, with many opportunities for study, but the greatest advantage was to have social intercourse with cultivated minds.

One can understand the dismay at Broad Lane when letters from Richard revealed that what was thought to be a good settled job for him was to prove so disappointing. Time and time again he petitioned the school committee to release him from his articles, and time and time again he would receive an anxious, loving letter from his mother trying to dissuade him from the course he was taking.

As early as May 1849, when he was still sixteen, Anne was writing to Richard: 'We received thine with one from thy master yesterday. It's with feelings of rather anxious character that I attempt to write, seeing that matters are come to an important crisis with respect to thy settling . . . .', and the first paragraph goes on to tell all from an anxious parent to an unsettled child:

.... for when we consider the many and great advantages connected with the situation you now hold, such as being placed directly under the care of kind friends, and that thy food and raiment is so nicely provided and money to procure any little comfort thou might desire besides, and then on the other hand when we consider our own circumstances as by no means being easy ......

The following April, the theme is still being pursued. They have had a sale at the shop and Joseph has done too much and is not well and she excuses him for not writing to Richard. He will soon .... 'I fear we shall not be able to find any place suitable for thee at home or abroad – besides I hope thou wilt be favoured to find satisfaction in thy present place.'

The following year, Richard's efforts prevailed and he was able to leave Sidcot, to venture bravely into the unknown world of commerce in the Midlands.

Apart from the nature of his character, Richard had few aids to help him. Only four foot ten inches tall, and with a very large head he was, at first sight, something of a figure of fun. He had, too, a slightly handicapped arm, one weak eye that was a serious handicap, especially socially, and rather a deep sonorous voice that belied his diminutive figure. Shorn of physical attributes to help him, he did not see himself as the man later described on his death as having a simple and direct manner of speech from the heart to the heart and able to address great audiences.

Indeed, arrived at Bristol and before taking train to Birmingham, and now so close to his old school at Sidcot, Richard did have a moment of painful doubt for, as he wrote later: 'With no business experience, and now face to face with life, I was filled with great terror, and it was my mind to go back to school.'

Now I turn to James and Joseph the two eldest of the family.

After leaving school James got a job at the Copperhouse Foundry, Hayle, where he began as a 'molliwog' (the boy at everybody's call). This did not bother him at all. He was thrilled to be in a proper workshop where great engines were made and where the swiftly acquired skills as his enthusiasm was noted, and more and more kinds of jobs were put his way.

He helped in the making of parts for the Clifton Suspension Bridge, and was on more than one occasion on hand when

Brunel made a visit to be present at the testing of key parts. It was this that first introduced James to the function of the hydraulic press which, before many years were out, he was to improve and, with his brothers, to build to such perfection that they saved Brunel's reputation. But more of that later.

The nature of this work at Copperhouse so captivated him that he was thankful for a disappointment he had suffered earlier. His father had obtained for him an introduction to the Perran Foundry from John Williams of Barncoose, the well-known mine owner himself. Taken by his father for interview, it was a great disappointment for him to be told that no one was wanted. Thus he went to Copperhouse. Many years later, before the end of the century, both Perran Foundry and Copperhouse Foundry were offered for sale to the brothers in Birmingham.

It was after Copperhouse that he went for a short time to a wheelwright, George Willoughby in Pool, for no other reason than to build himself a tricycle, but he stayed on. He learnt to make a wheelbarrow from stem to stern, and he could make a cart-wheel in two days. Though only a boy he could do everything of an equal quality to a man's work. His pay was fourpence a day, but his experience in woodwork gained in this primitive workshop was something that stood him in great stead later when he was able to make intricate casting patterns himself in the early days of the Birmingham works.

James was next employed by William Brunton senior, who had been one of Brunel's engineering assessors, and with one Edward Wilkins worked on an improved method of Brunton's dressing tin. Among other orders they fixed a set for St Ives Consols Mine, one of the oldest working mines in Cornwall.

This brings to mind an experience that George Tangye had when visiting St Ives Consols for an order some ten years later. The mine captain, Billy Daniel, pointed at an ancient-looking set of stamps worked by a water-wheel which was pounding away at the ore brought up from the mine. 'My father', he said, 'was a miner and captain here all his working life, and between the two of us we could reckon quite a hundred years of labour in the mine. During all that time those stamps have been called the 'Tangye Stamps', and the great shaft near it is called the 'Tangye Shaft'.' Until now I have been unable to unearth the origins of the part of the family that earned this connection with St Ives in the middle of the eighteenth century.

William Brunton, senior, had a private workshop in Pool, and it was here that James helped make for him some hydraulic pumps. In this workshop was a wonderful Holtzapffel lathe which James worked to great effect.

He was next engaged by the Redruth Foundry where he stayed for a year, and during which time he worked building one of the engines for the Hayle-Portreath railway, which subsequently became a familiar sight puffing over the railway line through his father's fields.

In his own time, inspired by the Holtsapffel lathe and the extension to his working skill that it provided, he set about building one for himself. It was this same precision lathe that he made that was later to be responsible for the first steps of success of the brothers in Birmingham.

James spent about a year at the Redruth Foundry, and then had an opportunity, which he took, to go to Distin and Chafe, general engineers, Devonport. He lost no time making his mark. One opportunity fell into his lap shortly after arriving. The manager was suddenly called away for no less than his wedding and honeymoon, when a difficulty arose about the design of a parallel motion of a 25-horse power condensing beam-engine which was being erected at Stonehouse. None of the men on the work, nor any of the partners were able to solve it.

James's experience in making his model engines had given him a thorough insight into this matter, and he modestly suggested that he was able to supply the required design, a proposal from the boy that was received with derision. However, the business was urgent and he was allowed to carry out the work which he did successfully. His wages here were from forty to sixty shillings a week, most of which he sent home to his mother.

Lay-offs had to be made by the Company due to shortage of orders; and because his landlady's son (John Ripper) was one of those who would have to go, James offered to give up his place and Ripper was not discharged.

James went home to Illogan and joined his brother Joseph who was working for William Brunton, junior, in his private workshop. The two brothers together formed a perfect partnership for development projects, one of which Brunton was pursuing at the moment in the field of fuses.

This partnership, which was at the heart of the subsequent success of Tangye's Ltd., was due to the almost saint-like characters of each of them, and the union of skills they each possessed. James Tangye, besides being an able designer of new tools, was an exceptionally able mechanic, and Joseph was a superlative craftsman. Each was linked to the other in their total dedication to steam engines, hydraulics, and all things engineering. To the gentle Joseph, brother James, throughout his life, could do no wrong.

At Brunton's their work was to develop machines for the improvement of fuse production methods for the Company— the Safety Fuse Company. No doubt this interested the two brothers especially, because their old grandfather, Edward Bullock, the same who was in charge of the largest of the three Tolgus mine engines, used to make fuses on a little machine like a lathe as the customer watched, but he never could make one longer than three or four feet. Later, Edward, a younger brother took out a number of patents for fuses he invented.

At Brunton's, they soon were able to make a fuse of any length required, and the speed in making it was only limited by the speed at which gunpowder could fall vertically.

Whilst at Brunton's, they manufactured lengths from two to three hundred feet for Sir John Franklin's famous Polar Expedition. It was of a special kind and covered in percha and produced for blasting at great depths of ice. George Tangye writes that he affirms that while engaged on this work Brunel, who was re-constructing the West Cornwall Railway, came to see them occasionally to view their various operations. William Brunton, junior, was then Superintendent Engineer of the West Cornwall Railway.

And now for a word on the younger of these two brothers, Joseph. James had been born in October 1825, Joseph was born thirteen months later. Joseph spent some time on his own with John Holman, where he got experience of boiler-making and other ironwork. The brothers were later together at the Redruth Foundry where Joseph worked the largest lathe. He was there accepted as a craftsman of the highest order, especially in metals. But he suffered from ill-health for a while, when he was engaged by Lady Bassett as a paid reader to the blind of the neighbourhood.

Before joining up with James at Brunton's, he had a spell, too, in Plymouth where he had been engaged on making the first match-making machinery for Bryant and Mays. George, the younger brother of these two, writes delightfully of these elder brothers at this time:

> James and Joseph worked in pair-harness – always together – but Joseph was the faithfull follower through all his simple and beautiful life, and in his eyes no human being could equal his gifted brother, James.

Both remained at William Brunton's for some years until the fuse works was established, for which they made all the machinery. Many workpeople were employed, and the two brothers became the working managers, remaining there until 1855.

However, to return now to Richard and his solitary arrival in Birmingham. A few weeks previously he had answered an advertisement that appeared in the *British Friend*, a Quaker paper, and he was offered the post of a clerk in the office of a small engineering works owned by Thomas Worsdell, whose father built the first railway carriage for the London and North Western Railway. He started work there on the following morning, immensely satisfied that he was part of a commercial business at last, but aghast at the difference in the scenery from that he had enjoyed at the only other place he had stayed in away from home, Sidcot. Here it was, winter and the streets were ankle-deep in mud. The 'works' were situated up a narrow lane in the smokiest and most grimy part of town. The office was in a loft, approached by a step-ladder. On entering he found his employer, wearing hat and overcoat, standing writing at his desk. He said, 'I'm glad you've turned up; will you copy these invoices?' All his fears vanished, and he felt happy that his entry into business life was in so unpretentious a place.

It was at this firm, Worsdell's, that first germinated the seeds that combined to grow into the Tangye Works, for George joined Richard in Birmingham less than a year later, in 1853, working for an iron founder, Eliot Hodgkin, as clerk of the works, and then, ten months later he joined Worsdell. In 1855 Richard persuaded his two elder brothers, the brilliant James and Joseph, to take the plunge, leave Cornwall and come to Birmingham to work for Worsdell, James as works manager, and Joseph to introduce a better standard of workmanship to the workmen.

So now four brothers were together. Their total salaries amounted to £400, so they took a house and all three sisters came to live with them to run the home. There was no one left at Broad Lane, for both parents had died.

Work at Worsdell's continued satisfactorily for all four brothers and business prospered swiftly, some hundreds of workers becoming employed, but after three years Richard had a disagreement with the most junior of the partners, and left.

At this point, I am going to digress along a rather sad lane which led to disagreement between two of the brothers nearly half a century later.

In 1904, George Tangye wrote, for private circulation, his *A Family Cruise*, telling the story of these early years in the brothers' fortunes. Being fairly readily available, it has been accepted by chroniclers as the standard account.

I have always had a copy of this little book, with its red and gold cloth cover in my library, but my copy is of rather special interest. In the fly leaf is written in George's handwriting, 'Richard Tangye, from the author, 14th March, 1905.' Nothing very particular about that you may think. But written through much of the book, in blue pencil and in Richard's handwriting, are signals of disagreement with what is said – exclamation marks, underlinings, crosses, question marks and protests 'Not true!' All these insertions reflect the disagreement by Richard with what is said about himself. Their tone is in sorrow rather than anger, and obviously the need must have been intensified by the note at the end of the book, 'This little narrative has my full approval – Signed, James Tangye 23 September 1904'.

I am impressed by the concern Richard shows for George, almost entirely forgoing any temptation to be angry with his sometimes wounding inaccuracies – for example his reference to the alleged fact that Richard was dependent on his brothers who subsidised him in terms of lodging and food. This was clearly not so.

And what is my authority for this? Quite by chance I found not so long ago a bound pamphlet which was the same size as George's booklet, and which I had vaguely thought in years gone by was a copy of George's *A Family Cruise*. The slight difference in title had not registered with me, namely *The Cruise of the Cornubians*. The authorship of George's book was ascribed to 'One of the Crew', whereas that of this other I had found was 'By One of Them', and 'this one of them' was Richard and was an answer to George's erroneous statements. Far from being a cantankerous riposte to his younger brother, the privately printed work was dedicated:

> To my brother George
> My inseparable companion and
> colleague for more than sixty years.

I have never before seen any reference to this work of Richard's, one so obviously generous in his attitude to the inaccurate George; and so I take pleasure in using Richard's account of those early days in Birmingham for the résumé that follows.

Before Richard was to leave Worsdell, he was responsible for a major innovation in industry for the improvement of working conditions, a subject he had in the forefront of his mind throughout his life, and one which made Tangye's Ltd the leader it was in this field.

At this time, when a young man of twenty, provincial newspapers were only published once a week, and in any case were too expensive for him, so he became a subscriber to a newsroom, paying a penny a week. During the spring of 1853 he read a series of letters in a Glasgow newspaper, signed 'Common Sense', in which the relations between employers and employed were discussed.

Amongst other things the writer strongly recommended employers to pay wages on Friday evenings so that the wives of the men were thus able to make their purchases by daylight on Saturday, instead of by flaming gaslight late at night when the best of everything had gone.

Richard drew Mr Worsdell's attention to this idea, together with a plan for working a 5½-day week instead of a 6-day, which was then universal practice. Both these plans were accepted by his enlightened employer, and it was not long before most other firms followed suit. In passing, I may say that one of his later achievements was that within a few years when there were 2,000 men at the Cornwall Works the payment operation was over in six minutes.

It was before he left Worsdell's that Richard was engaged in canvassing for orders and this led to his setting up on his own and starting out as a humble merchant himself selling goods of other people's manufacture. This, then, was the beginning of his true calling, a career which led the *Daily Chronicle* to record as being that of a 'self-made, energetic, enterprising man who became wealthy without shedding any principles, or losing his sympathy with the people from whom he had sprung'. And in this connection he had a passion for the development of education for all. This was reflected in the opportunities he afforded his workpeople, and the people of Birmingham as a whole.

The first of his visits to Cornwall after he had ventured on his solitary road to fame included a call on William Mayne. With his help he obtained orders from the West Cornwall Railway for a quantity of rivets. These Richard supplied through Bayliss & Co. And an uncle of his, Uncle William, introduced him to the manager of Dolcoath from whom he received some excellent orders.

It is illuminating now to quote from Richard's booklet, referred to above regarding George's statement on his dependence on his brothers at this time. Richard writes to George:

> *You say my little business was abandoned when I became a partner with my brothers* .... A stranger reading this would conclude that the brothers had been in partnership before I joined them which was not the case. We all joined the same time.

And, he might have reminded George, it was he, Richard, who was responsible for all of them coming to Birmingham, that it was this little business of his that started the commercial side of the family firm.

He goes on:

> The brothers had known I was struggling to get a little business together and cheerfully gave me my breakfast and

supper (my dinner was usually taken in town and paid for out of my small earnings) but had no money from them for my clothes or anything else.

On referring to my cash book of the period, which was audited and every page cast up by yourself I find that during the few months you erroneously say (to the contrary), I actually provided a sum out of my own earnings for the family chest, equal to half a year's rent of the house in which we all lived.

In 1855 James and Joseph set up on their own, Richard bringing business to them, all three working at Mount Street.

And here is another vignette of that period:

You say, *'Richard left his desk in town, and had another at his brother's office'*. You know perfectly well that Joseph had no office – he merely had one end of Pumphrey's packing room, and the 'office' was made expressly for me and consisted of an apartment four feet square, the walls of which were made of brown paper.

Into this same packing room, a revolving shaft projected to drive Joseph's lathe. The rent was four shillings a month.

Richard worked to find orders from far and wide. On one occasion he went to London, and seeing a screw jack in the window of John Vardon and Sons in Gracechurch Street, ventured in. After waiting patiently a couple of days he succeeded in being given an order for 72 screw jacks and 144 rigging screws.

His money was getting low, so he set out and walked half way to Birmingham, with the order in his pocket, passing through Barnet where the Horse Fair was on. This was an order for a merchant called John Williams, who, instead of being delighted with Richard, cut his commission by half *because it was such a large order*.

This ungenerous action was the spur for the brothers to make jacks themselves, and was the beginning of their trade in screw jacks and hydraulic jacks.

The title of this chapter is 'The Young Tangye Brothers of Illogan'. By purposely including in the title a parochial flavour,

I intended to convey the subject matter to relate to them as human beings behind the circumstances that led to their leadership of a great industry.

We have followed their development, up to the time of their partnership, and it is here, on the threshold of success, that I intend to leave them. Before finally doing so, however, we're going to join them timidly looking into a crystal ball which would throw some light on what the future held for them.

In this year, 1856, let us join them in their house in Spring Street, on the morning when, for the first time, no wage packets were going to be brought in at the end of the week. They were, for sure, anxiously waiting, waiting for something to happen – and it did!

Brunel had designed the huge iron ship, first called, while building, *Leviathan*. In 1854 she had been laid down on the southern extremity of the Isle of Dogs in the Thames Estuary, so that she was building throughout the same time as the firm of Tangyes was modestly being laid down in Birmingham.

She was designed so as to be able to steam to the Indian Ocean, and even Australia, perhaps, with 4,000 passengers and without refuelling.

She was 692 feet long, had six masts with 6,500 square yards of canvas and engines to turn a 24-foot diameter screw as well as 56-foot paddle wheels. Her displacement was 22,500 tons, not to be surpassed until the *Lusitania* half a century later.

Tremendous interest was generated throughout the world during the three years of building this giant; and when the time approached, in 1857, for launching her into the Thames, speculation and excitement by the public put pressures on Brunel that were enormous.

And no wonder – for how could he be sure of being able to push this 12,000 ton inert mass into the water, and with the whole world metaphorically watching, too? The *Quarterly Review* gave a good impression of it:

> The voyager up and down the Thames had noticed with astonishment the slow growth of a huge structure ..... At first a few enormous poles alone cut the skyline and arrested his attention, then, vast plates of iron, that seemed big enough to form shields for the gods, reared themselves

edgeways at great distances apart, and, as months elapsed, a wall of metal slowly rose between him and the horizon.

The Great Ship ...... although building in the midst of the largest collection of sea-faring people in the world, stands a wonder and a puzzle to them all.

The writer goes on to give a vivid picture of her size:

Nearly 700 feet long, from side to side she measures 83 feet, the width of Pall Mall. She could just steam up Portland Place with her paddles scraping the houses on each side.

When the day came for the launch there was a crowd of 3,000 to watch the ship slide down sideways into the water. The crowd was there having paid their money for tickets into the depleting coffers of the company. This was despite Brunel's horror at such a new and delicate operation being public; an operation which he was intending to orchestrate in complete silence so that instant orders could be heard by everyone in order to ensure integration of each man's task.

Came the first push. She wouldn't budge. Then two or three feet, and stop. No more. Fiasco. She even killed a man in a further decisive gesture of contempt. Shame and ignominy by a merciless public on Brunel.

The Field wrote:

Why do great companies believe in Mr Brunel? Is it because he really is a great engineer? If great engineering consists in effecting huge monuments of folly at enormous cost to shareholders, then is Mr Brunel surely the greatest of engineers.

For three months ignominy prevailed, futile attempts being made to move the ship down the slipway into the water while critics reviled Brunel, and his ship's proud name, *Leviathan*, was twisted and turned into 'Leave-her-high-and-dry-athan'.

For those in Birmingham, in the Tangye Brothers Mount Street workshop, all this was taking place in a different world, but no doubt James and Joseph had heard of Brunel's troubles with sympathy, remembering his visits to the Copperhouse and Brunton works.

Richard, too, sitting in his brown paper four-foot square office, with the business in screw jacks he had brought John Williams, must have given some thought to the great ship's undignified fate. He had walked 'hundreds of miles through the streets of Birmingham looking up this trade' for John Williams. Amongst other customers for jacks Richard secured for Williams were the merchants, Thornton and Sons, who gave orders for many screw jacks through him to John Williams.

Though Richard did not know it at the time, Thornton's had Brunel as a customer, so that it was natural that when James Tangye completed his first hydraulic jack, something well ahead of its time, Richard should take it to the firm he knew, namely, Thornton's.

Thornton's immediately brought this to Brunel's attention as a means of resolving the terrible impasse he was in with his recalcitrant *Leviathan*, now called *The Great Eastern*.

Thus it was, as Richard wrote:

> One dark evening in the winter of 1856, Brunel's agent came to our little workshop behind the baker's and rang the bell. I opened the door: but the gentleman apologised, saying he had made a mistake, and was moving away: but I could not afford to lose a possible chance of business, and so said, 'Whose place are you looking for, Sir?'
>
> He replied, 'Tangye's'. I told him he had come to the right place and invited him in, when, having told us his business, he was quickly re-assured upon seeing one of the machines before him. He ordered several of them – but James told him that the number of jacks he had ordered would not be sufficient to effect the launch, with which opinion he did not agree.

James, subsequently, was proved right. The boys from Illogan, the eldest still only 32, had come far. Where the whole engineering establishment had failed, they had succeeded in spectacular fashion; for they had launched *The Great Eastern*, and, with maritimely gratitude, *The Great Eastern* launched them.

And, I would add, gave to humble Illogan a permanent niche in the history of industrial progress.

VI

The Singular Richard Lander

The nature of the coastline south of Newquay changes dramatically, from the high cliffs to which we have become accustomed, to some miles of sand dunes stretching back inland, and sandy beaches of low profile. Even the names of features are placid; the Chick, Holywell, Penhale, Porth Joke, St Agnes. I notice, as we sail out of Newquay Bay and round Towan Head, Nun Cove. *Spray* ripples her way through a smooth sea, rising and falling in easy motion to a steady swell that could, strange to think, have been conceived six thousand miles away in the South Atlantic.

The lazy motion reminds me of the first time I saw her kind, a 30-foot wooden hull Falmouth Pilot, designed by Rodney Warrington Smythe, of Falmouth, for the man who wants to roam the seas in an ocean-going yacht, free of the chains of time in terms of hours and minutes, happy to share in the passage of time measured in centuries. From another boat I saw this Pilot class one coming out of Falmouth crossing my bow, this beautiful boat heeling to the wind, the sun glinting on her wet, varnished hull, gliding over the dappled golden sea, flecked with a thousand wavelet shadows; and in long due course *Spray* was built for me.

The beaches we have been passing, and are now going by – Watergate, Whipsiderry, Lusty Glaze, Fistral – are all the servants of the holiday-maker, the surf providing the joys of playful water, from the first innocent paddle of an infant to the sophisticated acrobats on surfboards who relish the thrill of riding it, with the sting of its lively record unconsciously providing the zest.

Many a vessel in a gale has been driven ashore, the crew and passengers at first thankful for being on sand, not rock, only to face the power of pounding surf against the wounded, wooden hull. As the tide rose on the stranded vessel, the breaking waves rose ever higher, forcing the crew to up into the masts and rigging. Here they could be for hours, cold, wet, frightened, wretched, while the piercing wind and thunderous waves maintained their brutal assault on the hull, worrying it, lifting and shaking it like stray dogs with a sheep. Ultimately, the hull might split, and the masts and rigging with the men clinging or lashed to them, would crash down into the turmoil. If they were not killed in the mêlée they would be drowned in the relentless power of the white and roaring surf.

It never fails to astonish me that in many parts of the world where there are long, long stretches of beaches and no harbour, ships engaging in trade lie off at anchor while their goods are transferred into local boats, which are then piloted and dexterously manoeuvred to shore through surf six foot high, maybe. The noise, a long sustained roar, is an awesome background to the delicate manoeuvres the local crew employ, marrying the weight of the load to the power of the sea drawing it to the beach on the broad shoulders of the surf.

One such area of coastline is the Bight of Benin on the West Coast of Africa. And some hundred and fifty years ago, a young Cornishman, born in the Dolphin Inn in Truro, found himself in one of those boats. He was on a very unusual mission.

On the morning of 23rd June 1834 a small meeting was held at Truro, to discuss a proposal of importance to the town.

The meeting proceeded smoothly, as was to be expected, and lasted barely half an hour. Three days later, there were delivered to each of those who had attended, a copy of the Minutes. Here they are. I ask you to read them, and then stay with me while we consider the courageous attainments of the subject of the meeting; the triumph and the tragedy of a young Cornishman of humble station, Richard Lemon Lander.

> In the chair, Humphrey Willyams Esquire. This meeting was held in pursuance of the Resolution, and the following address was presented and unanimously adopted.
>
> The lamentable fate of the African Traveller, Richard Lander, calls for some marked expression of public sympathy and respect; and more especially does it behove Cornishmen

to show their esteem and sorrow for their Adventurous Country-man.

Whether to testify the natural sentiment, or to declare our admiration at the energy of mind which raised the Departed and his Enterprising Brother from humble station to such an enviable pre-eminence, or to evince that deep interest which every Philanthropist and Christian must feel in all that concerns the civilisation of Africa, we are assured that there can be but one opinion as to the propriety of raising some lasting Memorial of the Travellers.

The effects likely to result from their discoveries, followed up to such indomitable resolution as characterised Richard Lander, may be inferred by the melancholy circumstance that this courageous man has, in all probability, fallen a victim to the suspicions of those concerned in the atrocious Slave Trade.

But the grand object has been accomplished, though great the cost; the path now opened for mercantile enterprise will make plain the way for civilisation, freedom and religion.

Park, Denham, Ritchie, Clapperton and Lander have led the 'forlorn hope' against the seemingly impregnable fortresses of African barbarism, and though each has perished, the cause of humanity has been enhanced.

At once, therefore, to celebrate the progress of discovery, and to record individual merit, it is proposed to erect a column in some conspicuous part of Truro, the birthplace of the Landers which, while it commemorates the melancholy fate of one brother, will render a just tribute to them both.

And to this end it is intended to apply the amount obtained for a testimonial of respect of another description (sic) which sum, however, being inadequate, the Committee appeals to the liberality of the County, confident that contributions will be immediately forthcoming to render the memorial worthy of the occasion.

Now let us see what this is all about. In our present century the primary area for explorations by science and astronauts is that of space. There is no question about that. Equally, there was no doubt in the nineteenth century that the rewards from the dangerous ingredients of exploration lay in Africa.

It may be surprising to learn that the relative intensities of danger, doubt and technical limitations can closely be compared one with the other. This may be apparent when the time factor is considered, and the length of time the participants are exposed to unknown factors, unknown except in one sense, that they are hostile and potentially lethal.

At the time of writing the longest period that an astronaut has been in his hostile environment has been less than a hundred days, while Richard Lander on his last of three expeditions, one that proved fatal, was nearly a thousand days in hellish conditions of uncertainty, not just from natives and wild beasts, but from an almost invisible enemy, fever from insects, that struck and killed mercilessly.

The symptoms of this fever did not vary very much. The victim complained first of giddiness, slight pain across the forehead and at the back of the eyes, then of a quickening pulse, a tongue becoming white and red at the tip, obscure vision, rapid reduction in strength, vomiting of a dark coloured substance, and great thirst. After the first few hours the patient appeared anxious to avoid contact with anyone, no matter who, and remained in his hammock or crept off to some isolated corner. If asked how he felt he would reply that he was quite well and denied suffering any pain.

About the third day he would become delirious, and from between the fourth and the ninth he would be likely to die. The current treatment had been hardly soothing, the patient having been cupped and blistered, his head shaved and cold lotions applied, purgatives administered, and later six to ten grams of calomel every four or five hours. A robust man was bled up to thirty ounces.

The expectancy of life for the African traveller was very low, far lower than that of the modern astronaut explorer. I repeat this rather surprising fact as it gives a further dimension to the courage and endurance of the Victorian travellers, on their long, hazardous trips in hostile country, hostile natives, hostile animals, hostile weather conditions.

In the meantime, let me continue with my attempt to prepare the reader with enough information for him to get all he can from my narrative of one of Richard Lander's three journeys exploring the Niger river, the main gateway to West Africa.

A picture is given by R.A.K. Oldfield, who went with Lander on his third and last expedition. The object of all these expeditions was entered in his Journal by Barclay Fox after he attended a meeting in Exeter in 1840 of the African Civilisation Society. At this time, he states, 500,000 slaves a year were being exported, a vast trade in exploiting helpless humanity, and the Society had as its aims:
1. To commercialise
2. To civilise
3. To christianise.

Much of its power lay in the fact that there was this twin endeavour, the betterment of trade and the eventual abolition of the slave trade, so that merchants and philanthropists were united in the same overall endeavour, to open up the Dark Continent, to let the light in so that what had been hid for centuries could be open to the world. It was just not the white man who was the slave trader, but the African too, the existence of slavery and worse being part of native culture.

This union of interest between philanthropy and commerce was explained by Oldfield in this way: 'In the hope that the attempt recorded in these volumes *(Journal of the Niger 1832)*, to establish a Commercial Intercourse with Central Africa, via the River Niger, may open new fields of enterprise to the Mercantile world, and of usefulness to those who labour for the amelioration of uncivilised man ...'

One day while the expedition of three vessels was fitting out at Milford (having abandoned doing so at Liverpool because of cholera there) Oldfield was standing on deck watching the crew of the *Alburkad*, one of two steamers, mustering. He looked at the fine young men as they got into place. There were twenty-five of them, and Oldfield wondered to himself how many would return safely.

Three years later, he knew the answer. Only three, and Oldfield himself, survived. One of those on the expedition had been its leader, Richard Lander. He was not there. He had been shot by a native a short time before leaving Africa. Only three out of twenty-five; and yet, throughout the century, the Royal Geographical Society was busy sponsoring, or advising expeditions who traversed Africa, opening it up for Europeans; but whether the native subsequently benefited is another question.

And if the world will benefit from the incursion of the traveller into space is yet to be determined.

Of Richard Lander's early life in Truro we do not know much, but he left us with some knowledge in his introduction to his *Records of Captain Clapperton's Expedition to Africa*. In this he tells us that as far back as he could remember he never wanted to stay in one place long.

He was born in Truro in 1804, the fourth of six children, on the very day on which Colonel Lemon was elected to Parliament, 'and owing to this striking coincidence, singular as it may seem, my father who was fond of sounding appellations, at the simple suggestion of the doctor who attended the family, added *Lemon* to my baptismal name, Richard.'

Nothing, he says, remarkable occurred in the first five or six years of his life, but early in his youth his rambling inclinations began to display themselves. He was never easy in his mind unless he was on the move, playing truant and strolling from town to town, village to village. He sought the company of boys possessing the same restless habits as his own, and he used to listen avidly to old women's tales about the manners and ceremonies of natives in different regions of the earth. Their marvellous descriptions of monsters existing, they affirmed, in remote lands, likewise raised in him a longing to be a traveller.

The tales he listened to, no matter how incredible they sounded, made a deep and permanent impression on Richard, and when very young, he had already made a firm resolution to become a wanderer. Incidentally, he gives an interesting insight, at this point, into the rather unexpected attitude of the matronly tellers of tales to whom he listened. 'These venerable matrons of my native country,' he writes, 'moving in the humbler walks of life, are fond of the wonderful, and endeavour to stamp a love of it in the tender mind of youth with all the solemnity and earnestness of age and belief.'

The restrictions of family life led to friction within the home and even led Richard 'to leave my family home at the age of nine, and ever since I have been almost a stranger in the place of my nativity.'

Though we do not know the circumstances that led to the next dramatic event in his life, he 'accompanied, two years later, some gentleman to the West Indies, and whilst in San

Domengo caught the local fever and nearly died, only being saved by the kindly ministrations of some benevolent negro females.'

After an absence of nearly three years he returned to England (1818), and then surprisingly continued in private service for the next five years, during which time his employer took him to a number of countries on the continent.

Returning to London from one of these trips, he learned that a Major Colebrook, one of His Majesty's Commissioners of 'Inquiry into the State of the British Colonies', was in need of a servant to accompany him abroad. They left Portsmouth on 13th February 1823, and after a stormy and hazardous voyage of no less than five months finally dropped anchor in Simmon's Bay, South Africa.

Richard attended on the Commissioner during a tour of some months, and then left his service to sail home, arriving in England in 1824 when he joined the Customs Service. And now we come to the beginning of his comparatively brief, but brilliant career as one of our greatest explorers, one who would be much better known than he is were it not for his humble origins, and the contemporary snobbery of the geographical establishment in the nineteenth century that subtly diverted the spotlight away from him.

Hearing that a new expedition was currently being planned for the purpose of finding the source, the route and the termination of the mysterious river Niger, Richard obtained an introduction to the leader, Captain Hugh Clapperton, a man who had already led an adventurous life at sea, both in the Navy and in a merchantman from which the Press Gang in Gibraltar hauled him when one day he was on shore leave. He was put to serve on a frigate in which he saw action off the Coast of Spain sustaining a head wound which always gave him trouble. He appears to have been in the Navy some ten years, seeing service in the West Indies and even in Canada.

For a while there was a pause in his active contribution to life and, on returning to England, he lodged with an aged aunt, embellishing this sanctuary by fathering an illegitimate son (born in 1819).

His adventuresome spirit them led him to Tripoli as companion to a Colonel Warrington, then the Consul, and together they explored the nearby desert. It was then that he first went into West Africa, on orders from the Colonial Office. They sent him out to go overland from the Bight of Benin, where the slave trade was being carried out to an enormous degree, to Sokoto and to try and record the course of the Niger. He returned to England a very weak man.

As Richard set out for his interview he went over in his mind the reasons for his wish to exchange the security of Truro with the outlandish hazards of distant exploration. Though his reasons did not readily come to mind his motives were quite clear, and being instinctive left no room for reason to shake them. The number of casualties that had befallen members of earlier expeditions were very real in his mind, but nothing could dislodge from his mind the charm he found 'in the very sound of the word Africa'. It made his heart flutter on hearing it mentioned, 'whilst its boundless deserts of sand; the awful obscurity in which many of the interior regions were enveloped; the strange and wild aspect of countries that had never been trodden by the foot of a European, and even the very failure of all former undertakings to explore its hidden wonders, united to strengthen the determination I had come to, of embracing the earliest opportunity of penetrating into the interior of that immense Continent'.

Captain Clapperton could only have been a poor character indeed if an antipathy at their first meeting was to deflect Richard from his earnest ambition. Any danger of that, however, was completely swept away. Though some twenty years older than the applicant who stood before him, Captain Clapperton was attracted by his unusual force of character that revealed itself in his dark, solemn eyes, and quiet strength of personality that showed through his efforts to gain acceptance by the leader to take part in his expedition.

Richard, on his part, already a great admirer of the captain from a distance, had not expected to meet someone to whom he would feel an immediate attraction, and from whose eyes a fire and an energy seemed to scintillate, as question and answer were exchanged. He would serve the captain at any cost, and was most happily rewarded with the appointment, by Clapperton, of Richard as his confidential servant.

This engagement drew immediate entreaties from his friends

and relations to reconsider it, to cancel it whatever the cost, for the hazards were too great, surely he must know that? The chances of survival were minute.

Richard received numbers of letters from his relations in Cornwall that tried to represent convincingly the emotional disadvantages that his decision would have if he failed to accede to the entreaties of his friends. These pleas were as ineffectual in dislodging him from his determination, as the medical warnings that doctors gave him, and statistics displayed.

Among those who endeavoured to influence him in this way was George Croker Fox, the head of the distinguished Fox family of Grove Hill and Penjerrick near Falmouth. To all these kind and earnest supplications Richard warmed, but they moved him not. That he was not deceiving himself into disregarding the warnings from all these good people is starkly shown in a phrase he used when referring to them as dangers ahead of him that in their letters 'they justly dreaded'.

Still worrying about Richard, Fox wrote again promising to procure for him a more lucrative situation in one of the south American Republics, but nothing would make him change his mind. Instead, with joyful heart, he accompanied Captain Clapperton in a post-chaise driving down to Portsmouth through pouring rain. On the following day, 27th August 1826, they embarked on the *Brazen*, a vessel of some 200 tons, and awaiting them were other members of the party: Captain Pearce, RN, an amiable individual to whom Richard took an instant liking. Unfortunately, the Captain was to prove too delicate for the arduous task he had undertaken. Then there was a naval surgeon, Doctor Morrison, another doctor, a Scotsman called Dickson who had served for a long time in the West Indies. In attendance on the party were Columbus, a West Indian mulatto, who had accompanied Major Denham on the most recent journey to the Niger, and Pasko, a coloured native of Haussa.

A light breeze eased the *Brazen* out into the Solent, and slowly she made her way up toward the Needles, the breeze on her beam helping her smoothly out into the open sea. The expedition was truly on its way.

There followed many days of inactivity during which Clapperton and his colleagues discussed the possibilities that lay ahead for the party, giving Richard, with every day that passed, an increase in his knowledge of likely conditions of the terrain and the customs, habits, character of the natives, potentially and naturally hostile to these white intruders.

Every contingency was allowed for which might help appease the chiefs of the tribes they would encounter. A considerable store of gifts was carried with the purpose of oiling the wheels, where suspicion, or even hostility, might cause friction.

None doubted the dangers that faced them when making contact with a chief. Their potential for brutality of a horrifying nature existed long after the period we speak of. The wives of chiefs suffered, surprisingly, perhaps, more than most, for when her husband died, one of his wives was chosen to be sacrificed. This was done in different ways by different tribes, none worse, surely, than that told by Oldfield (on Lander's third expedition) about an occasion they witnessed when the chosen widow was tied to a heavy log and left on the beach. She could not free herself from the log, nor could she drag it for it was far too heavy. She was left like that to allow the incoming tide to float it and be taken out to sea by the outgoing tide to where the sharks would devour her.

Dorothy Middleton, in her delightful book *Victorian Lady Travellers* gives another aspect of tribal horror, that of cannibalism. Mary Kingsley was one of her Africa Lady Travellers she writes about. Like a number of these female explorers she was a woman of tremendous energy and independence and waltzed through danger and discomfort with swirls of her voluminous skirt. Throughout her journeys through jungle and desert and native villages enshrining innumerable hazards, Mary, like other lady travellers in the nineteenth century, always wore 'her stout Victorian skirt and prim head-dress, and carrying the umbrella with which she prodded hippopotami and took marine soundings'.

It is hardly surprising from this picture of her that she took cannibalism in her stride, even going so far as to liking particularly among the natives the Fans who 'were known to eat human flesh, not as some tribes did in religious ritual, but as a staple article of diet'.

Though cannibalism was to be prevalent in certain areas for a long time to come, the ancient custom of human sacrifice was on the wane. As far back as 1833, Oldfield was writing with approval that human sacrifice was being replaced by goats on such occasions as the death of a chief, but this was by no means universal, as Lander was to find out.

Oldfield goes on to remark about this improvement as it 'shows they are getting ashamed of their religion ...' Referring to the trade engendered by the magnitude of the slave-trade at the ports along the coast of the Benin Bight he declaims 'that such a state of society should exist where British trade has been carried out to an enormous extent and for a considerable time, may well excite astonishment in those not aware of the diabolical influence which the slave-trade exerts both by the enslaved and the enslaver'.

Those on board the *Brazen*, though sympathetic to such a condemnation, and hopeful their expedition would leave behind a contribution toward its diminishment, nevertheless were more interested in the task in hand. As they sailed south they called at Porto Santo on the smallest island of the Madeira Islands. Having obtained various samples of plants and minerals they sailed on to Teneriffe, which they reached five days later on 13th September 1825.

Here at Santa Cruz Richard had a taste of the unexpected casting the first shadow over the future of the expedition. Captain Clapperton went ashore, with three of the officers, to climb up the mountain, the main geographical feature of the island. This they had to abandon for Clapperton felt suddenly ill and, after a rest, they all had to return to the boat.

Richard was shocked by this mishap to the Captain. Over the days that had passed since leaving Portsmouth, the confines of shipboard life, and the common adventurous purpose, brought intimacy quicker among the party than would be the case for strangers on land. Richard had come not only to admire his leader, his integrity, his strength of purpose, his modesty, but, above all, his considerate manner and warmth which inspired and evoked a love that all leaders must hope for and few attain.

The news that his hero was ill acted as a blinding light that brought the future and its possibilities into focus. Fervently he hoped that he would be able to give all the support to Captain Clapperton that he might need, even in the dark moments that he saw would come.

On the 16th the *Brazen* sailed again. After she had called at the Cape Verde Islands for a brief stop she sighted a small schooner which she chased and, in due course, closed and over-took. Her reason for doing so was to see if she had slaves on board, in which case she would have been later reported, if she were British, to the authorities. It turned out she was Russian, bound for Pernambuco, so she was allowed to proceed.

A little later, on the 8th, another sail was spotted, and suspecting also that she was engaged in the nefarious traffic in slaves, they pursued and boarded her, only to find their suspicions confirmed. They discovered 196 slaves in this French schooner, each chained to another, and crammed between decks in a horrifying manner. Between decks there was only about three feet in height so that this mass of individual human beings had to remain in a sitting posture the whole time they were onboard, which could be many weeks crossing the South Atlantic Ocean.

Lander was one of those in the party that boarded the vessel. The visit was made as short as possible, for the stench exuding from this confined space was overpowering. He was greatly affected by the fate of these wretched people, but was powerless to do anything for them, so hastened back aboard the *Brazen*.

Resuming their journey southward, this spectacle they had just seen, this witnessing at first hand the reality of the detail in this inhuman trade (half a million people a year taken away from this land and their birth – *Barclay Fox Journal*) brought the subject well to the fore of those onboard the *Brazen*, and for the first time Richard concerned himself with it, resolving to do all he could toward contributing to the aim of outlawing the shipowners of Portugal, of Spain, of France, of Holland, yes, and of England, too, those particularly of Liverpool and Bristol who made themselves rich from this traffic in human misery.

Henry Kingsley, a Fellow of the Royal Geographical Society, tells in his book *Tales of Old Travel* (1871), an authenticated account of the process of buying and shipping the slaves in the period at the end of the seventeenth century. This is some 130 years before Richard Lander dropped anchor in the *Brazen* off the slave-trade coast of Africa. Things had not changed much, there being, as he saw on his next voyage, fourteen Portuguese vessels lying off at one time each waiting for the slaves to arrive from the interior, and each capable of taking perhaps 700 slaves.

The price for a good man slave was 100lbs weight of small cowry shells, between three and four pounds in money. Before purchase, the slaves were rounded up amid scenes of despair and brutality, and each one examined by a surgeon paying particular attention to his teeth, there being no other way of guessing the age.

As soon as a slave (man, woman or child) was passed by the surgeon, he was branded with a hot iron with the ship's letters in order that it might be known when finally handed over. A few days after, the goods agreed upon were paid for, and the slaves were sent to the 'trunk' or collecting paddock.

When some fifty or sixty were collected, they were marched down to the shore, and got through the surf in a long boat. On arriving on board the men were at once put in irons, two and two together, to prevent mutiny, or swimming ashore.

The negroes are so 'wilful', as one captain, hardly compassionately, put it, 'and loth to leave their own country, that they will leap out of the ship, and stay under water till they are drowned' sooner than go to Barbados, 'which they dread worse than we do hell'.

The slaves are all prisoners of the internal, tribal wars, which are made expressly to obtain them, wars that are often more bloody because of the resistance to capture. Each individual was fighting for himself, not for a greater, lofty, tribal aim.

When the whole complement of slaves was made up the ship would commence her voyage westward across the ocean, to the West Indies or the Americas. Let us just consider one ship, the *Hannibal*, Captain Phillips, trading for the 'African Company' carrying negroes to the West and bringing gold and ivory from Africa home.

The *Hannibal* was a vessel of 1,300 tons with a crew of 80. Normal capacity for such a vessel would have been 200 passengers; instead she carried 750 slaves (480 men and 220 women). The voyage started in calm conditions, very hot, of course, and with no ventilation from a breeze finding its way down below through a hatch. In eleven days they had only gone 750 miles, about a quarter of the straight line distance. They had not even cleared the great shoulder of Africa. The negroes, stifling in the holds down below, began to die, and the confidence of sharks following the ship was well repaid.

After being at sea sixty days, sails still flapping in the hot light airs, the first case of cholera occurred, and in its most awful form, too.

There were few recoveries. Once seized with it, the victim was given up for dead. At the same time cases of smallpox appeared, and for the next two months the plague went on unchecked. By the time they arrived in Barbados, 14 crew and 320 negroes had been thrown overboard to the accompanying sharks.

The 'African Company' was susequently distressed at the news of such a voyage, not saddened by the loss of life, but on account of the commercial loss to the Company. This was £6,500.

No, one need hardly feel sorry, and there was quite a large section of the public at that time, both individuals and welfare groups, who shared this contemporary view of ours, and who actively worked toward the time when the trade was forced to stop.

However, the general view at that time can be exemplified by the public remarks of two gentlemen. One was an Alderman of the City of London, and his opinion is recorded for all to see in the *Parliamentary History, Vol XXIX*, p.343, but to assuage your eagerness to go so far as to look it up, let me quote from it to save you trouble.

This Member said, 'The abolition of the trade would destroy our *Newfoundland* fishery which the slaves in the *West Indies* alone supported by consuming that part of the fish *which was fit for no other consumption*, and consequently, by cutting off this great source (of demand) would annihilate our marine (fishery).'

The Reverend John Newton who, incidentally wrote a 'Life' of his namesake, Isaac, gave a different view. In 1763 he wrote, of the slave trade in which he had previously and personally been engaged, 'It is indeed accounted a genteel employment (sic), though to me it did not prove to be so, the Lord seeing that a large increase in wealth could not be good for me.'

On 29th November the *Brazen* arrived safely at her destination, dropping anchor in Badagry Roads. No time was lost in making final preparations so that the equipment which was to be carried inland by the expedition could be checked, and the expedition speed on its way.

Among the equipment assembled on deck was a very important group of packages that, in fact, had nothing to do, *per se*, with anything the members might require. These were the vital gifts that would have to be handed to the chiefs from whom favours and safety were asked for. The drain this had on the expedition's limited carrying capacity can be gauged by the gifts Lander thought expedient to give to 'King' Boy alone. For the sake of accuracy I must interpolate here that this list refers to Lander's second expedition.

It was as follows: fifteen or sixteen guns, 2 barrels of powder, 15 soldiers' canteens, knives, spoons, soldiers' coats, some tobacco and rum.

It would seem imprudent, to say the least, to provide the guns and powder, but since the Portuguese first landed in Africa in the sixteenth century, firearms had been valuable currency for services and obviously the explorer and merchant must have felt the risk was worthwhile. In Lander's case, it proved otherwise, for when he was attacked and mortally wounded on his third expedition in 1830, it was a bullet that hit him, not an arrow.

Apart from the presents, there were further items to be taken to placate potentially hostile chieftains; by flattery and by something very near debasement, if the verbose addresses are taken at face value. One should, I suppose, call the sentiments expressed as being dictated by the need for diplomacy to counter down-to-earth reaction from the lips of a man who might playfully ring your neck. Anyway, they make interesting reading as giving a vivid picture of the fragility of the relationship at its outset.

The one I have before me is elaborately written in Maghrubi script and is one that was taken by Richard on his last expedition. Presumably, on presenting this to the Chief on entering the territory, he read it out in an English version from which I quote now. If my reader gives it his attention for a few minutes I believe it will be worth his while as it illuminates, indirectly, the extraordinary isolation of an African explorer's situation, and his dependence on those enjoying a savage and primitive culture:

Praise be to God, Unique and Alone: There is no power nor might save in God.

From God's lowly servant, Richard (Lander) .... followers of his Highness, the ruler of the English State, perfect peace (to you) greetings and respects.

To our beloved, mighty in God's power, the prince and ruler, master of this land, Peace be upon you, God's mercy and His blessings. To proceed, following these expressions of regard and esteem; we advise you – May God cause you to know all good – that His Royal Highness has sent his followers and subjects a number of times previously to the lands of Northern Africa for the purpose of beholding and discovering their marvels, their seas and rivers and the strange things that are to be found in them, things not to be found in our land.

When the subjects aforementioned returned they informed him of the favour, kindness and bounty, pious conduct and protection which they had met from you and the people of your land.

You had openly and freely declared to them that they could bring to your ruler goods, wares and commodities for sale and for the purpose of commerce and trade and that over them was God's safe keeping and protection ...

We are accompanied by and carry goods from among those in our country for the sake of transaction and barter for the tooth and tusk of the elephant, and the feathers of the ostrich, and for wax and for other of the goods of your land which are not found with us ... We shall pay to customary dues and give gifts as is current in the commerce of your markets ...

Then follows a long passage of more lip service and flattery, but conveyed in such a brilliantly modest way that I can well imagine the toughest of chieftains to be impressed.

But I am wrong to treat this document in any way as something to be amused by, for the African Traveller knew what he was doing by this time so far as projecting his image to the best advantage on the natives was concerned, and to suggest otherwise is unworthy. Though it served as a passport for a journey of 1,200 miles on foot or canoe, it failed in the end to keep the bullet away from killing Richard Lander.

That is ahead of us. Here we are considering the first of Richard's expeditions, and the members of it are now on deck in Badagry Roads ready to get into the boats that will take them ashore through the tall, tumbling surf to the beach of this, the Dark Continent.

Richard wrote touchingly of this scene:

> The day after the arrival of the *Brazen* at Badagry, the gentlemen of the mission and the officers of the ship assembled on the quarter-deck to take a final farewell of each other; and some of the latter were deeply affected, as with a faltering voice and agitated manner they breathed their hopes that success might attend the perilous undertaking to which their enterprising friends had so willingly devoted themselves.
>
> There was something so moving in the pathetic spectacle of Englishmen parting under a strong persuasion, almost amounting to a conviction, of meeting no more in *this* world; in seeing the manly resolution and stubborn indifference of British officers combating with the tenderer and more amiable feelings of human nature, that I myself could only with difficulty stifle my emotion; and to dispel the gloom that hung upon my mind, I bade the officers a hasty and respectful adieu, and shaking hands with many of the honest seamen on deck, I sprang into a canoe.
>
> As two of the natives were rowing it to the shore, I took the opportunity of playing 'Over the hills and far away', on a small bugle horn which I had brought with me. This elicited the admiration of the sailors of the ship, and I landed amidst the hearty cheers and application of them all.

A canoe which followed Richard's did not meet with such an easy passage. It was, indeed, the image of the plight of this canoe during its journey through the fantastic surf of which I was reminded when watching, from *Spray*, the Atlantic surf plunging toward Perranporth Beach.

The canoe was taking Mr Houtson, an English merchant, from the *Brazen* with a number of delicate astronomical and other instruments. When it was where the surf was at its highest the canoe was swamped, hurling the luckless occupants into the foaming water, buried for what seemed an age in the surf which stretched in white glory for miles along the coast on either side.

An eye-witness recorded at the time that Houtson and the crewmen were buried in the foam of the waves, and then reappeared when two of the black crew saw that Houtson was in real trouble. In fact he was unconscious as they, fighting against the thunder of the waves, somehow struggled with him to the shore where he was helped into consciousness again.

Subsequently, the natives, expert divers, managed to retrieve all of the instruments, which was surely miraculous. Unfortunately, all but a few were ruined by the damage from the water.

The canoes referred to above were built purposely for this heavy task of transport from ship to shore and *vice versa*. They were of immense size and very strong with very thick hulls and manned by nineteen men.

Each trip was undertaken to the accompaniment of a ritual. A 'Fetish-man', covered from head to foot in *gris-gris*, stood in the bow invoking the 'spirit of the waters' to be propitious and quell the fury of the sea. When he thinks his petition has been heard, catching a favourable opportunity, he claps his hands in a transport of effort and exclaims, with violent exclamation and wilfulness of manner, 'I-yaw, I-yaw!' (now is the time!) which inspires the crew to fresh energies, stabbing their paddles into the water. In this way the enormous vessel is propelled through, and down, and with the waves 'with the swiftness of lightning'.

Now had come the time for the expedition proper to begin, the time to follow up the planning and the empty hours of anticipation on the long voyage, and to plunge into the interior of Northern Africa where all manner of harsh experiences awaited them as they well knew.

Clapperton and Lander, with Doctor Morrison, and young Captain Pearce and Houtson, were likely to be called upon to render on many occasions all the courage, ingenuity and endurance they could muster, while ever hovering near would be the evil spectre of fever, shapeless, invisible, silent, its random touch enough to kill within a few days.

I am not, in these pages, intending to act the narrator of Captain Clapperton's expedition, but rather to dwell on moments of it, and thus show reason why we should be proud of Richard Lander, the young man from Truro, who chose to explore where no white man had ever trod.

On 2nd December the party arrived at Badagry, having crossed the river Formosa, which was a mile wide, which gave an idea of the scale of things that lay before them. Here they had their first confrontation with a Chief, an exhausting and anxious affair.

The 'King', Adolee, sent Captain Clapperton a present of a bullock, a fine pig and some fowls, and the following day he arrived on a visit in all the pomp and barbarous magnificence of African royalty. He was mounted on a diminutive black horse, and behind him and around him and in front, everywhere, there were more than a hundred subjects dancing and singing to musicians playing instruments which Richard said were of the 'rudest' description. The king was gorgeously arrayed in scarlet cloak covered with gold lace. On his head was a turned up hat with more gold lace and an ostrich plume surmounting it all.

A further feature of this delightfully out-of-place display was the accompanying escort of two boys in black cocked hats, each with a musket in his hand, on either side of the horse's head, while a dozen or so of his wives stood around their lord and master with one of them coming forward to hold an unfurled umbrella over the great little man, who was by now squatting on the ground.

Richard took this to be a suitable moment to unfurl a Union Jack and hoisted it over him. The warrior chief was as pleased as a little girl might have been, but it was the man in him who ordered rum to be handed round with him taking the first quaff of what was to prove a long session.

The party continued with music, and shouting and dancing, culminating in nothing less than Richard playing English and Scottish airs on his bugle horn.

The next meeting they had with a chief, started in the same sort of bizarre fashion but did not end so smoothly. On this occasion the travellers were brought to his residence where, during the parley, his young wives could be plainly seen stealing peeps at the white men through holes in the walls, but when it was realised what they were doing they ran off very confused.

Near the entrance to this 'town' they saw for the first time a 'fetish-hut', a large one with a number of wooden figures carved in bas-relief, some in a kneeling, some lying down, all outside the walls. These were the idols the people worshipped and to which they ascribed miraculous powers. A feature the expedition welcomed was the belief that the land surrounding it up to a certain distance was sacrosanct insofar as any goods placed on it were in the hands of the gods and could not be touched by anyone but the owner.

At an early hour on the following day, the chief was in a surly mood and alleged that he had not received a present proportionate to his respectability or expectations. Consequently he declined to make any effort to procure anyone to convey the baggage which was very necessary to the expedition, some dozen men being required. Captain Clapperton, however, somehow succeeded in borrowing a horse, and he and Mr Houtson would ride it in turns.

In the evening the party set off in the twilight, a trying march in the darkness ahead of them. It was very rough going, the path winding through the forest exposed to dangers from both man and beast.

To add to their misery, Captain Clapperton was rubbed sore due to riding this narrow-backed, thin horse without a saddle. It became so painful that he had to get off and walk though he was wearing only slippers. Unable to keep these from slipping off he had to stagger the remainder of the way bare-footed. His feet began to swell and blister, so that before reaching Isako, the next resting place, they were literally bathed in blood.

Arrived at their destination they found their precious baggage had gone on to Dagnoo, and that they had to go on to be with it. Seeing their plight some friendly natives came to the rescue and led them by torchlight over the intricate path which was nevertheless a most trying ordeal.

At midnight they arrived, clothes torn, worn out with fatigue, only to find there was no shelter and they had to sleep out in the open. They had done this once before, waking up completely drenched by the dew, a feature they feared would bring on a fever. This time, they again awoke drenched.

They moved on next morning, early, to Humba and there found Captain Pearce and Dr Morrison accommodated at the chief's residence. Shortly after arriving, absolutely dead-beat, Clapperton was taken ill, but staunchly insisted that they went on to the next village though he was weak and only just able to walk.

Misfortune was still their companion, for the baggage carriers, they had found, were now being detained by the local chief until a flask of rum was given him by way of tribute. This man, with a leopard skin slung over his shoulders, came up as soon as he saw the arrivals and insisted he had the rum. Eventually, he was satisfied with a glass of grog prepared for him by Houtson. The chief consumed this in the most extraordinary way.

Instead of swallowing it, he adroitly squirted it into the mouths of his faithful attendants. They stood, mouths open, eyes expectant, eagerly waiting to receive the liquor thus so deliciously refined. It was relished by all.

Two days later, during which another wide river was crossed with difficulty, the party was in poor shape. Morrison, Lander, and Captain Pearce all being taken ill, all had to be carried in hammocks by native bearers.

The party, making for Katunga, the capital of Yariba (still some three hundred miles away) was being decimated, but still, in spite of the onslaught of fever, still managed to marshal the strength of mind to continue. They were only three weeks out on this expedition expected to last eighteen months and more, when Dawson, another young member, fell ill. All were now ill in varying degrees. During the night, hearing Dawson's groans, Richard asked him how he was. Receiving no answer he went to his bedside and found him a cold corpse. The sight of so ghastly a spectacle made Richard shudder and give a shout of horror which woke Captain Pearce who murmured that he had not long to survive and then sank back exhausted.

Dawson was buried the same evening, to the fearsome lamentations that had been noisily made all day by the natives. Indeed, Richard said of their ritual that as soon as they heard of the death they set up their death-yell, and that if all the friends of darkness had joined in chorus, they could not have produced an effect more frightfully and fearsomely appalling than was the sound produced in that instance.

There were now only three Whites left, and their outline of resolution began to blur. Nevertheless, after it was clear that Captain Pearce had rallied a little, they set off again in more cheerful spirits.

For three days they journeyed through country that could have been England, and where the natives were especially friendly. All seemed better, much better, and the future once more beckoned with the breath of assurance.

Then . . . .

About eleven o'clock Captain Pearce became suddenly worse, and an hour or two later was delirious. He talked much and incoherently, in detached sentences; at one time apparently conversing with his mother in the most affectionate terms, asking her questions, answering them himself, and then the next moment reverting to his own melancholy condition. In this pitiable state he remained until nine o'clock in the evening when he fell into a stupor. Later, attempting to raise himself up, with a faint groan, and a convulsive shudder, he fell back and instantly expired.

Captain Pearce, a Naval Officer of spirit and charm, with a 'gentle and pleasing manner', had rendered himself a valuable friend and close companion to the two survivors, Clapperton and Richard, so that his loss was a devastating event when taken within the context of the situation in which the remnant of the expedition found itself. His wit and cheerfulness were to be most sadly missed, and Clapperton would have had every excuse if he had surrendered to the fate which had befallen them. The news that followed swiftly on this, shocking though it remained, was diminished in its intrinsic horror by the deadened state of the survivors' spirits. The news was that Dr Morrison, who had gone on to the next town with Mr Houtson, the trader on his way back to the coast because of his fever, had also died, and at almost the same hour as Captain Pearce.

So now there were left just two, Richard Lander, of Truro, and Captain Hugh Clapperton. Before them lay the planned trek of hundreds of miles inland on foot. Every step offered danger, from fever, wild animals, weather and natives. Even to the well-equipped, those fortified by the camaraderie of companions, it would be hazardous in the extreme. For the two survivors, hearts heavy with loss, the spirit could not be strong enough to face it. And they were both feeling ill, too, so no one could blame them.

But they did not think that way. They had set out to widen the door into Africa, to attract attention on the iniquities of the slave trade. And, by God, they would do just that. Or die.

And now, as they used to say in the cinema travelogues, we bid farewell to our heroes for some ten months, during most of which time they were separated with hundreds of miles between them, Richard in the Kano area, Clapperton further north in Sokoto. Clapperton's task of fostering friendship with chieftains, with future trading in view, and the studying of a large area, was made particularly difficult and dangerous by the inter-tribal war going on, a war in which horrifying things were done and cannibalism was rampant. Space does not permit me to linger, which is perhaps just as well. Instead, I pick up the story on 1st April 1827, when the two explorers meet again, Richard having come up to Sokoto from Kano.

During this time of being apart, each had borne the aching pain of living dangerously with the unknown, and the isolation of one from the other. This long period of uncertainty had had the effect of binding the friendship of the two men into love and respect for each other, though Richard could never think of Clapperton as being anything but his 'master' and would never think of himself as anyone but his servant.

Clapperton greeted Richard warmly, the more so as Clapperton had been unable to move away from Sokoto for many weeks owing to the restrictions placed on him by the circumstances occasioned by the war. He was killing time, waiting for it to be finished, so that he could convey the King of England's greetings to each of the opposing chiefs, a delicate mission one might with reason concede. But now he had a companion, Richard, and they would make the most together of their enforced idleness.

However, a cloud hung over them in the form of neither feeling well. Richard described his health as tolerable. He had never felt in perfect health for a single day.

Each of them spent a lot of time on shooting in the vicinity, or hunting as the natives would call it. Clapperton, much keener than Richard, would leave with his gun at an early hour and might not return until evening. On all of these occasions he dressed himself in local style which consisted of a large flowing robe and a red cap with muslin turban. The robe was drawn into his waist by a broad belt in which two pistols and a short dagger were stuck. He seemed to appreciate looking like a robber setting out on a robbing mission, a change from the neat demeanour of the British naval officer. He enjoyed a further flamboyant attribute, namely, a beard of truly patriarchal length and the envy of the Falatahs who attached great importance to beards.

The two men had to themselves a round building about thirty yards in circumference, having a very small entrance so that from the outside the building looked like a beehive. It had no window so that all the light they had was what came through the little opening. The heat was appalling, being ten degrees higher than in the shade outside. It lay in a square yard where at one end the horses were kept, the other the camels. Sheds were erected close to it to accommodate the slaves.

Each evening was the occasion for nostalgic talk and songs, 'Home Sweet Home' being the favourite of the Falatahs listening outside with breathless attention to the music of the white-faced strangers.

Anything that reminded Clapperton of his native Scotland filled him with emotion. A little poem, 'My native Highland Home', was sung by Richard many, many times as Clapperton squatted opposite, his arms folded on his chest, listened with a tear in his eye and thoughts that could not hide the feeling he would never see home again.

Thus were their lonely evenings spent. For two months their routine was rarely varied; and then, on 12th March Clapperton fell very ill with dysentery, and a punishing routine for Richard began without pause, the only person to care for his 'dear master'. No one would assist.

From the moment he was first taken ill Clapperton perspired in the form of large drops of sweat continually rolling over every part of his body which badly weakened him. Apart from normal nursing Richard had to counter the effect of the appalling heat on his patient by fanning him for hours together; in fact, all his leisure moments were occupied with this tedious occupation, only stopping when the fan literally fell from his hand as the result of fatigue.

On 15th March he at last persuaded an acquaintance to lend him one of his female slaves, and this he did. The girl began well and cheerfully, but soon ran away and never returned. All this time the suffering patient had to endure a temperature of 107 degrees at noon, and 109 at three in the afternoon.

Clapperton earnestly wanted to write, but when Richard brought him pencil and paper the mere action of sitting up exhausted him and he collapsed back onto the bed.

The two men tried to keep their spirits up, but it was very difficult. They were isolated, out of reach of all help to stem the disease, while they were also in a savage environment combating, as best they could, not only the onslaught from this disease, but the emotional despair at having failed; to have come so far in their great undertaking and for it to end thus, was a shattering disappointment.

Richard's exertions and situation cost him dear, for they had weakened him enough for a fever to take hold which later was almost to prove fatal. But that was not to be. Instead the inevitable happened.

On the morning of 13th April 1827 Richard awoke and was greatly alarmed at hearing a peculiar rattling noise in his master's throat. At the same time, his breathing was loud and difficult.

Richard wrote later of these lonely moments:

> ... My master, calling out 'Richard!' in a low, hurried, and singular tone. Observing him ineffectually struggling to raise himself on his feet, I clasped him in my arms, and whilst I thus held him, could feel his heart palpitating violently.
>
> His throes became every moment less vehement, and at last they entirely ceased. Insomuch that thinking he had fallen into a slumber, or was overpowered by faintings, I placed his head gently on my shoulder, gazing for an instant, on his pale and altered features. Some indistinct expressions quivered on his lips, and whilst he vainly strove to give them utterance, his heart ceased to vibrate, and his eyes closed for ever!
>
> I could not bring myself to believe that the soul which had animated it with being a few moments before, had actually quitted it.
>
> I then unclasped my arms, and held the dear hand of my master in mine ...... Oh God! What was my distress in that agonising moment? Shedding floods of tears, I flung myself

along the bed of death, and prayed that Heaven would, in mercy, take my life!

But heaven was not listening. Instead, God gave him strength to face his hard duty, to find his way home, without help, alone; so that the records of their journey could be safely delivered. Hopefully, others who followed would benefit, and even the slaves might hear an echo from the tolling bell for the end of the traders' loathsome profits.

His duty was clear. He had to start the journey back to the Coast, there to await, hopefully, the arrival of a homebound ship that could take him on board. And that could not be less than *nine hundred miles away*.

This lonely journey, starting in the rainy season and through hostile environment all the way, was completed nine months later. I choose two experiences that Richard endured during it which will serve to convey the testing time to which he was put on that hazardous trek.

One evening, he had retired to rest in the hut that had been granted him as he passed through, when he was awoken at about midnight by a long, piercing shriek. Springing up from the ground where he was lying, he drew aside the lightly woven mat that served instead of glass, and looked out. There was a bright moon and everything was flooded with light so that he could see everything. A group of people were standing no more than ten yards away from him and among them were two women struggling violently to get loose from being restrained.

On shouting at them a futile request for them to stop, a man bounded across and told Richard that the women were two of the King's wives who had incurred their master's displeasure, and that it was nothing to do with Richard.

It was then that he suddenly realised he was to be a witness of their execution. Screams persisted, and then the women's hands were bound, then their feet. Lastly their heads were bent roughly backwards and then held tightly in that position by men pulling down on their hair.

Their last cry caused Richard's blood to run cold, it was so terrifying an expression of terror and anguish. Then, in an instant daggers were thrust into their chests, their throats were cut, and all was silent but for a faint gurgling sound like water issuing from a bottle.

'As soon as this bloody tragedy had been enacted,' Richard related, 'the spell that had bound me motionless to the window, dissolved and, flinging myself on my mat, I endeavoured to obtain a little repose, and calm the agitation of my mind . . . . . .' Next morning he was strolling through the town when, to his horror, he came upon the bodies of the murdered women hanging on the fetish tree.

The other scene I shall relate is not so horrific a spectacle, but was an appalling experience for Richard. On nearing Badagry, the coastal town from which the party had surfed ashore from the *Brazen*, Richard was thinking much, in sad reflection, of the decimation of the party that had set off into the hinterland from there with such high hopes.

Now he was the only one left. His master, Captain Clapperton, cheery Captain Pearce, Doctor Morrison and Dawson, all of them dead. The thought of them, of their comradeship which had been dispersed so swiftly, made him yearn to get to Badagry to see a white man and to speak with him. Thankfully, he was nearly there. Only another week, perhaps a day or so more, and he would be there. Little did he know what lay between.

One morning, when he was taking his breakfast of Indian corn and palm oil, he was startled by a message from King Adolee commanding him to appear at noon at the fetish-hut and be examined by the priests to answer charges that would be brought against him.

A crowd had collected on hearing of a white man's arrest, and its appearance was frightening, for all seemed to be armed with axes, or spears, clubs or bows and arrows. Inside the fetish hut a number of priests were assembled. After preliminaries, one of these cried out loudly, 'You are accused, white man, of designs against our king and government, and are therefore desired to drink the contents of this vessel which, if the reports are true, will surely destroy you. If they are not true, then you have nothing to fear: the fetish will do you no injury, for our gods will do that which is right.'

The ritual was fearsome for Richard, all eyes being on him in deadly silence, magnifying his ordeal into what seemed a preview of a judgement in hell.

'I took the bowl in my trembling hand,' he wrote, 'and gazed for a moment on the sable countenances of my judges; but not a single look of compassion shone upon any of them. A deadly silence prevailed in the fetish house, this gloomy sanctuary of skulls.' Seeing no possibility of escape, he swallowed back the potion, and threw the chalice on the ground. From the expression on the dark, still faces around him, those present expected his swift collapse, but it was not to be, and silently they rose and made a way for Richard to pass through, a free man.

Later, he was told the liquid he had been forced to swallow was a concoction made from the bark of a tree, and that he was the first for a long time who had escaped its fatal attention. It had a disagreeably bitter taste, and apart from causing slight feeling of dizziness for a short while, left no lasting effect.

Arrived at Badagry, Richard had to wait two months before a vessel appeared. This was the *Maria*, which took him to a British naval ship, the *Esk*, and on her he embarked on the 13th February 1828. He disembarked at Portsmouth on 30th April, bringing with him the news of the main artery of the Niger delta, the river Nun.

Richard remained in London for four weeks, and then, after an absence of thirteen years, returned to his home town, Truro.

An entry in the H.M. Customs Oath Book for the 30th June 1829 shows Richard Lander being sworn in to the Department; and the Board's minute of 16th November of the same year states that 'Richard Lander, Weighter of the Third Class' was allowed leave of absence for fifteen months as he had been recently engaged by the Government to proceed into the interior of Africa. This was for his second expedition with his young brother, John, as amateur and companion.

Another minute of 29th December 1829, gives a list of articles required by Mr Lander for this journey, to be shipped aboard the *Alert*.

To us, who have followed his fortunes with Captain Clapperton, this list bears a familiar stamp, the means for purchase of goodwill toward the traveller from a not yet civilised 'bureaucracy'. It still makes interesting, colourful reading. It includes 90 yards of cloth (red, in all probability), quantities of razors, scissors, knives and combs, 30lbs of glass beads, 10lbs needles, 100 Dutch pipes, 200 dollars, 2 fowling pieces, 2 pistols and medical supplies. Incidentally, the latter calls to my mind the beautiful medicine chest, complete with bottles and ingredients, belonging to Richard Lander which is on view at the Royal Institution of Cornwall's museum in Truro.

I come close to the end of my short study of one period in Richard Lander's life. He was yet to make a third journey of exploration into the same huge area, a triumphant journey in that he completed his discovery of the course and outlet of the great and mysterious Niger river. It was a tragic journey, too, for he was mortally wounded in an ambush, but, God be praised, not before his goal had been reached, and not before he attained the right to be remembered as one of the bravest of the early explorers of that Dark Continent, Africa. He lies buried on the island of Fernando Po.

And now a postscript that adds further pride to Cornwall's contribution to the geography of distant lands.

If you have occasion to visit the Royal Geographical Society in Kensington Gore, you will see on the wall of the Lobby the list of distinguished holders of the Society's Gold Medal. The first man to have the honour to receive this medal is recorded as Richard Lander of Truro; and then, some 150 years later in 1978, is writ the name of Robin Hanbury-Tenison, of Cardinham, a brilliant explorer in our modern age. And that is yet another story.

For Lander's letter to the King, William IV, see Appendix.

VII

John Harris: the Miner, the Heart and the Song

It is now seven o'clock, and *Spray* is only five miles from Land's End. The sun is on its downward path, already gathering features of the sky together for the final glory of the day, sunset. The great orb itself is still bright, but a soft haze reduces its golden magnificence of this morning into a pale gleam. It is strong enough, though, to mark a gently dappled pathway of yellow gold across the sleepy water relaxing in rivulets after a day's varied display. On either side the colour of the water is apple green, muted.

A mile off to port is the coastline, along which, just here, are some of the most spectacular cliffs in the degree of their varied contours and colours, of anywhere along the coast.

The wind I had expected has not materialised. Indeed, all the elements appear as though they are combining to make the end of our journey as idyllic as one could wish.

Among the books I have onboard at the moment is one written in 1851 called *Rambles Beyond Railways*, and consists of 'Notes in Cornwall taken a-foot'. The author is Wilkie Collins who rambled enthusiastically along the coast distanced far from railways indeed, for the Tamar bridge was not opened until 1859.

One of the places he visited was Botallack Mine, one of the most extraordinary in Cornwall, a large mine right on the edge of the coast with galleries under the sea bed stretching out under the ocean.

On *Spray*, I am looking out for this complex of Victorian engineering and ingenuity, as I am intrigued after reading Collins earlier on.

We were told to go to the counting-house, and on our way thither beheld the buildings and machinery of the mine literally stretching down the precipitous face of the cliff, from the land at the top to the sea at the bottom.

Looking down we beheld a scaffolding perched on a rock, far below us, that rose out of the waves – there a steam-pump was at work raising gallons of water from the workings in the mine every minute, on a mere ledge of land half-way down the steep cliff-side. Chains, pipes, conduits, protruded in all directions from the precipice; rotten-looking wooden platforms, running over deep chasms, supported great beams of timber and heavy coils of cable; crazy little boarded houses were built where gulls' nests might have been found in other places . . . . .

Well, now I am looking across the water at this over the lines of swell that smoothly lift *Spray* and let her down again, as each unbroken wave moves shoreward under her, swiftly and silently. There, on those precipitous cliffs, I can see what remains of this extraordinary mining achievement.

For what it was like for the miner below ground I turn to a miner himself to tell us:

Below were caverns grim with greedy gloom
And levels drunk with darkness: chambers huge
Where Fear sat silent, and the mineral-sprite
For ever chanted his bewitching song;
Shafts deep and dreadful, looking darkest things
And seeming almost running down to doom.
Rock under foot, rock on each side,
Rock cold and gloomy, frowning overhead
Before, behind, at every angle – rock.

Here blazed a vein of precious copper ore
Where lean men laboured with a zeal for fame,
With face and hands and vesture black as night,
And down their sides the perspiration ran
In steaming eddies, sickening to behold . . . . . .
And Danger lurked among the groaning rocks
And oftimes moaned in darkness. All the air

> Was black with sulphur burning up the blood.
> A nameless mystery seemed to fill the void,
> And wings all pitchy flapped among the flints
> And eyes that saw not sparkled with the spars
> Yet here men worked on stages hung in ropes
> With drills and hammers blasting the rude earth,
> Which fell with such a crash that he who heard
> Cried 'Jesu, save the miner!'

Great stuff, and I would like to quote more from it, but we have other songs to hear from this miner, this poet, this family man, John Harris (1820-84) of Troon, near Redruth. I shall be intoducing him to you soon, but first, let me show you his other side, his love for nature. This is how he felt one winter's day on a visit to Penjerrick:

> I first beheld it when the wintry clouds
> Were rolling grandly through the murky air;
> And flocks of starlings, wheeling to their home
> Like sound of many waters, murmur'd there.
> Here graceful trees, the green, the rich, the rare,
> So chastely grouped in fairy fringes stand;
> And limpid rills and crystal waterfalls,
> And breathing song like notes from angel-land,
> Old Winter here is reft of his command.
> Red roses bloom, and fragments fill the breeze,
> Here forest-birds from off a friendly hand
> Pick their rich meal, and flutter 'neath the trees.
> If such, Penjerrick, be thy winter scene
> How Eden-hued in summer's flashing sheen!

John Harris was the eldest of ten children, and symptomatic of the precarious nature of life in those days, his earliest recollection is one of a little white coffin in which his eldest sister was carried to the grave.

He was born on 14th October in a builder-built cottage with reed roof, bare rafters and clay floor, locally known as the 'Six Chimneys', on the top of Bolennowe Hill, Camborne. One of the unusual features of the little house was that the woodwork of the roof was such that you could see the stars through the thatch. I do not propose here to go into details of his childhood beyond saying it was one of nature, of seasons and crops, of love and sunshine, and death, too, without fear nor favour; and of Sunday School and preachers, and loving parents and humility.

His father was a miner at Dolcoath, and life was so naturally confined to the necessities of survival and the gifts of nature within small compass of the homestead, that John did not see the sea until he was ten years old. And Portreath was only some seven miles away.

At the age of ten he started work on the surface at the mine, dressing and preparing copper ore for despatch. His day began with his leaving home at six in the morning, and the work was very hard. 'Sometimes,' he writes, 'I had to wheel the barrow full of mineral until the skin came off my hands, and my arms were deadened with the heavy burden so that I could scarcely put one foot before another. Sometimes I was scorched with the sun until I almost fainted, and at others I was wet ... Yet I never complained, nor would I if the same sharp scene had to be enacted again. God had placed me there and I knew that it was right.' He never got home from this long day of toil until six in the evening.

Referring to this period of his life he introduces the place that poetry had found in his life. All the time he was working 'I had,' he wrote, 'the song-angel to comfort me, walking at my side among the mineral splinters, rocks and rubbish, and whispering in the narrow lanes and grassy meadows as I travelled homewards, sweeter utterances than language can reveal.'

He goes on:

> On my way to and from the scene of my labours through long lanes bramble-covered, and over meadows snowy with daisies, or by hedges blue with hyacinths, or over whispering carnes redolent with the hum of bees, the beautiful world around me teemed with syllables of song.
>
> Haste, lovely lark, arise to meet the Morn
> That opes her dewy eye above yon hill
> Haste, sooty blackbird, to the flowery thorn;
> Haste, gilded linnet, to the purling rill.
> Come Contemplation, who dost love to dwell

> Where Solitude sits silent in her cell.
> Come soothing muser, listen to my sigh
> As o'er the fragrant heath I take my way
> To mark with joy the bursting dawn of day.
> And hark! the drowsy night-god murmurs by,
> Dull sleep awakes, the lowing kine are up;
> The sun looks forth from yonder streaky sky.
> I hail the golden orb, and onward life
> To drink the wine from morning's fragrant cup.

Not great poetry, maybe, but what a precious joy to summon for a young miner as he faces a day of telling toil, trudging across the heath on his way to work.

And work! At the age of fourteen his father took John down the mine for the first time, and just pause for a moment to visualise what this phrase actually meant. Dolcoath mine at that time was sixteen hundred feet deep. A shaft, of which there was more than one, was the way a man got down to his working. Instead of seeing this as a shaft going down into the bowels of the earth, imagine it a vertical channel going up a mountain sixteen hundred feet; and then imagine eighty or ninety ordinary ladders in this channel fixed one on top of the other. How would you like to climb up that, rung by rung to get to your work? To work chiselling rock for eight hours, and then climb down sixteen hundred feet by ladders, any false step, or misjudgement, or weakness leading you to inevitable death? And then, *doing it in the dark*, with only a candle on your helmet, secured only by a handful of clay, to help you? And have three miles to walk home?

That is how the prospect must have seemed to young John on that first day as a 'man' at the mine.

> My father went before with a rope (he wrote) fastened to his waist, the other end of which was attached to my trembling self. If my hands and foot slipped from the rounds of the ladder, perhaps my father might catch me, or the sudden jerk might pull us both into the darkness to be bruised to death on the rocks.
>
> Sometimes the ladder went down through the middle of a huge cavern, warping and shaking at every step, and with the

candle stuck to my hat crown I could not see from side to side.

Sometimes they slanted one way, sometimes another; and sometimes we had to climb over craggy rocks crashed into the void where a slip of the foot would be our doom. And when at last we reached our working place, a huge cell in the hollowed rock, I looked up in boyish expectation to see the moon and the stars, and was quite disappointed to find nothing but the blackest gloom. Foolishly I picked up a stone to see if I could strike the far-away roof, which rebounded back nearly upon my head. This silly experience was never repeated.

But the climbing up evening after evening, that was the task of tasks! Ladder after ladder, ladder after ladder, until they seemed interminable, and the top one would never be reached. Panting and perspiring, after stopping again and again, we reached the top at last, where the pure air of heaven fanned our foreheads and filled our lungs with new life, though our flannel dress could not have been wetter if immersed in a river.

And to think enduring that experience was not just a 'one-off' job, but one that John Harris and all his mining colleagues had to do every day of a six day week, the day being divided into three shifts of eight hours each, six days a week.

For twenty-three years he suffered this hard toil, the first of his tasks being wheeling the slabs of mineral from his father's working along a narrow level to the shaft. Here he tipped it onto a pile which was then put into a bucket and drawn up to the surface.

The level was very uneven so that the barrow, which had a lighted candle-stick stuck in the front end, often slipped from my hands.

Some of the corners, too, were very jagged and abrupt, against which I struck my joints, knocking off the skin until the blood ran down. Child as I was I had made up my mind not to cry; but the tears forced themselves out of my eyes upon my face, which I wiped away with my clayey fingers, and tugged and pushed at the heavy barrow.

A passage follows that today we can at first only think of as overdoing the sentimental to an extent of even overdoing the sentiment. Nevertheless, if we take the trouble to read it in the context of the verse that follows, it becomes touchingly sincere. 'I thought of my mother's smile,' John muses, 'the welcome which awaited me at home, and the dear bower of heather where I should watch the moon rise by and by; and I struggled on in my mining yoke, chanting quaint couplets of new-made rhyme to the echoes of my cavern:

> Today I've thrashed an old tin-rib
> Till I could thrash no more
> While streams of perspiration ran
> Unchecked from every pore.
> A fire-cloud drank my spirits up:
> How longed I for the breeze
> The hoary-headed woodman quaffs
> Among the forest trees!

The years rolled on and, difficult though it is for us trying to cope with the comparative ease of modern life to believe it, John became 'inured to my severe toil. But the Muse,' he wrote, 'never left me above ground or below.' Indeed, the Muse was the great solace of his life, that and his devotion to Christ.

'In the dust and sulphur of the mine I was making lines to jingle, impelled onward by a strange power I could not resist.' He would sew leaves together for paper. After a day's work he would walk the three miles home with his father, his father in front while he was quietly putting his thoughts together trying to rhyme, and writing notes in a corner of the kitchen as soon as he got home.

After a while he began to carry paper and pencil in his pocket, and jotted down his ideas as they came to him. Sometimes he would slip into a field and write under a hedge so as not to be observed while his mates from the mine walked on and left him. He would keep his paper and pencil hidden out of sight in his coat-sleeve, holding it there with the tips of his fingers. He realised his desire for solitude made him a little conspicuous but he always avoided giving offence. This was an attitude that went with him throughout his life. Always he wanted to shun the crowd.

Poetry (he wrote) was everything and in all things – the great unspoken inspirer, ay, the upholder of my life. I rushed to my verse-making no matter how exhausted I was by the mine. Every sheltered nook and green recess from Stony Lane to Brea River witnessed my rhyming struggle. The day broke and evening deepened, summer and winter refreshed my boyhood and youth, the true tongue of the seasons thrilled me with never-ending themes. This was my life-work for the weal of humanity, and by His help I would perform it.

There is a charming poem of his whose simplicity and genuineness is enhanced if, while reading it, one visualises from whom the memory comes of this time, none other than a miner, a labourer from the depths of the earth, who had spent the long day in circumstances as far from a place that one would expect a poet to be as could be imagined.

Two little girls had been born to his wife Jane, and mother and father got the utmost joy from them. Years later he wrote this:

The Faces at the Pane

Where'er I go, whate'er I do
A vision meets my eye,
From the far valleys of the past,
Flecked with the summer sky.
It comes in days of quiet trust
It comes in wind and rain,
It comes when harvest crowns the earth,
The faces at the pane.

When toiling in the darksome mine,
As tired as tired could be,
How has the glad thought charged my soul
My children watch for me!
And as I ope'd the garden gate
Which led into the lane,
How danced my heart to see once more
The faces at the pane

Two little girls with gleaming eyes
With soft and shining hair

And sweetest prattle on their lips
Were watching for me there.
One in the grave is sleeping now
And one has crossed the main
Yet still I see, where'er I be
The faces at the pane.

And when I brought some hedgerow fruit,
Or darling hedgerow flowers
Which they were taught to love,
Their kisses came in showers.
O, precious were those distant days
Which may not come again
Made brighter, fairer, fresher for
The faces at the pane.

I give the poem in full, not expecting it to be acclaimed technically as the poem of a master, for that it obviously is not. The more significant ingredient of a poem is the initial depth of feeling that prompts it, and this simple effusion from a hard-pressed Cornish copper miner must surely kindle a glow in the heart of all who read it.

This contrast between the sensitive human being above ground and the brave stoic of a man working all his days in the dark nearly two thousand feet below ground is something for all to marvel at. The life of John Harris, obscure and unknown to all but a few, is open to us through his poetry. My reason for presenting him in this book to you is so that the bushel covering the light from this little known Cornishman may be moved to one side a little more, and the light freed to shine onto a wider readership.

As one reviewer wrote in 1882 two years before his death: 'He is a living signpost to others along the way to success, and absolute proof – if proof be wanting – that genius is as much a gift of the poor man as it is of the rich man, and that it buds and blossoms as well in a humble cottage as it does in a luxurious studio, or a castellated mansion.' The literary *Athenaeun* declared his poems to be a 'phenomenon even in our own age – earnest, strong and sweet with a father's love and all domestic affections.'

For my part I just relish the comapny of this poet of nature, this delightfully sensitive rhymester, this loving parent with his unsentimental faith in God.

I cannot do better than let him bid us farewell with a splendid Kiplingesque rallying cry for all of us:

> Courage, weary workers!
> 'Tis not always dark,
> Comes the welcome morning
> Sings the soaring lark.
> Eat your food with gladness
> Aiding Nature's plan;
> Give the world a whistle
> Do the best you can!
>
> Plough the straightest furrow
> Pull the strongest oar
> Never mind the hardship
> When you reach the shore.
> Ever in your efforts
> Aiding Nature's plan;
> Give the world a whistle
> Do the best you can!

*

Yes – do the best you can. Well, *Spray* does just that. Hidden obstacles, not only rocks and wrecks, face us all and no doubt lie along *Spray's* track in future. Indeed, we are approaching now the first of them, the Longships reef off Land's End.

I would hope we shall make Falmouth by about midnight before the tide begins to ebb. Perhaps we will, maybe we won't.

Anyway, one thing I am sure of – *Spray* will do the best she can.

Appendix

The Petition of Richard and John Lander most humbly sheweth that we Your Majesty's loyal and dutiful subjects were employed by Your Majesty's late Government in an expedition to trace the course of the River Niger to its Termination, wherever it might lead. That having suffered many distressing privations and encountered numberless hardships and difficulties in the prosecution of this enterprise in which our lives were placed in imminent danger, and in which our healths suffered very materially, at length by the blessing and good providence of Almighty God we completely succeeded, after we had been plundered, captured,and sold for slaves by the natives—thus Determining a great geographical question which had been disrupted and agitated for many ages previously. --- That on returning to this Country with impaired Constitutions we feel the severest disappointment in not having been placed in situations to which we humbly conceive ourselves entitled for the important service we have rendered the Country, at the risk and hazard of our lives. But though our desires are by no means ambitious, we are still, may it please Your Majesty, without employment or the means of support, and we are consequently unsettled and unhappy. We therefore pray Your Majesty to recommend us to situations of some kind, by which we may be placed beyond the reach of want or the fear of poverty, convinced that Your Majesty will answer the prayers of the humblest of your subjects, as well as attend to the addresses of the mightiest.

And your petitioners will ever pray etc. etc.

To His Most Gracious Majesty the King at Windsor.

This plea was followed by an audience with the King lasting one hour and a half at Windsor on 9th February 1832

BIBLIOGRAPHY

Account of Thomas Pitt, 2nd Lord Camelford, An, G. Wilson. *The Eccentric Mirror,* vol II, London, 1813
Autobiography and Poems John Harris, Adams and Co., London, 1882
Barclay Fox's Journal, ed. R.L. Brett. Bell & Hyman, London, 1979
Beginnings of the English Newspaper, The, Joseph Frank, Harvard University Press, 1961
Bibliotheca Cornubiensis, Courtney and Boase, Vol II, Longmans Green, London, 1878
British Channel Pilot, J. Hobbs. Charles Wilson, London, 1859
Brunel's Three Ships, Bernard Dumpleton. Colin Venton, Melksham, *c* 1975
Chapters in the History of the Provincial Newspaper Press. D.F. Gallop, County of Avon Library, 1954
Collectania Cornubiensa, Boase, Netherton & Worth, Truro, 1890
Cornish Characters and Strange Events, S. Baring-Gould, John Lane, London, 1909
Cornish Magazine, Vol 1, 1898. Interview with George Tangye
Cruise of the Cornubians, The, Richard Tangye, Privately printed 1905.
Dolcoath, T.R. Harris, the Trevithick Society, Camborne, 1974
Douai Dairies, Catholic Record Society Journal, 1906
Early Cornish Printers, Journal of the Royal Institution of Cornwall, Part III, 1963
English Newspapers, Vol I. H.R.F. Bourne, Chatto &Windus, London, 1887
English Notes for American Circulation, Richard Tangye. Privately printed, 1895.
English Social History, G.M. Trevelyan. Longmans Green, London, 1942

Family Cruise, A, George Tangye. Privately printed, 1904
Friend – Recollections of James Tangye, The, William Bellows, c. 1910
Half Mad Lord, The, Nikolai Tolstoy, Jonathan Cape, London, 1978
Harris John: Lays from the Kine, the Moor and the Mountain; London 1853; The Land's End, Kynance Cove and other poems, London, 1858, a Story of Carn Brea, 1863; Luda, 1868; Monro, 1879; Linto and Lancer, 1881
History of Cornish Mail and Stage-Coaches, Cyril Noall, Bradford Barton, Truro, 1964
History of Cornwall, Vol III. Polwhele, Falmouth, 1803
Hundred Years of Engineering Craftsmanship, A, R. Waterhouse. Tangye's Ltd, Birmingham, 1957
Institutions at the Cornwall Works, Birmingham, 1884
John and Richard Lander, Notes on, W.H. Treggellas, Vol 6, Journal of the Royal Institution of Cornwall, Truro, 1881
John Norden's MS, Maps of Cornwall, facsimile, University of Exeter, 1972
Lake's, Parochial History of Cornwall, Vol I. Joseph Polwhele, Truro, 1867
Lanherne, Oldest Carmel in England, George W.F. Ellis, Bodmin, c. 1940
Lives of the English Martyrs, Dom Bede Camm. Burnes & Oates, London, 1905
Narrative of our Expedition into the Interior of Africa, Laird and Oldfield, Bentley, London, 1837
Naval Side of British History, The, Callender. Christophers, London, 1924
Newspaper Press, Vol III., James Grant, Tinsley, London, 1871
One and All, Sir Richard Tangye, S.W. Partridge, London 1899
Portreath, Some Chapters in its History, Michael Tangye, St George Printing, Camborne, 1968
Rambles Beyond Railways, Wilkie Collins, Richard Bentley, London, 1851
Records of Captain Clapperton's Last Expedition to Africa, 2 vols., Colburn & Bentley, London, 1830
Reminiscences of Travel, Richard Tangye, Samson Low, London, 1870

Richard Lander's Journal, 3 vols, London, 1833
Royal Cornwall Gazette, 1801-1900
Sailing Packets to the West Indies, The, British West Indies Study Circle, 1973
Sir Richard Tangye, Stuart Reid. Duckworth, London, 1909
Some Notes of the Tangye Family, J. Francis Parker. Privately printed, 1972
Songs from the Earth, D.M. Thomas, Lodenek Press, Padstow, 1977
Story of Glendorgal, The, Nigel Tangye, Bradford Barton, Truro, 1890
Story of the West Briton in Nine Reigns, The Claude Berry. Truro, 1955
Tales of a Grandfather, Vols I, II, III, Richard Tangye. Privately printed, 1897-1902
Tangye, Anne: Journal (1830-45)
Transactions of the Plymouth Institution, Vol XIX, 1943-44 and 1944-45
Victorian Lady Travellers, Dorothy Middleton, Routledge, Kegan Paul, London 1965
Young Man's Journal and Review, The, Interview with Richard Tangye. London, February 1895
British Library, Departments of Manuscripts, Printed Books and Newspaper Library
Birmingham Reference Library Collection, 1918-1931
180 Obituary Notices (75 columns) on Sir Richard Tangye, October et seq. 1906.
Richard Lander's Letters to the King, 1831 DDX70/7, Cornwall County Record Office

Index

Adolee, King, 155
Africa, 130-157
Agar, Mrs 104
Alaska, 45
Alert, 156
Alexander the Great, 26
Aliva, Vice-Adm Don, 83
Allen, Dr, 62, 63, 64, 66
America, United States of, 80, 87, 141
American Independence, War of, 38
Anne, Queen, 29, 35
Appledore, 11
Arthur, King, 16, 19
Arundell, Bridget, 75
Arundell, Thomas, 75
Arundell family, 57
Ashburton, 92
Athenaeun, 166
Atlantic Ocean, 11, 140
Australia, 41, 126

Badagry, 143, 145, 155, 156
Barbados, 141, 142
Baring-Gould, S., 26
Barncoose, 118
Barnet, 125
Barnstaple, 58, 61
Bassett, Lady, 121
Beacon Cove, 77
Bedford, 68
Bedford, Duke of, 85
Bedford, Earl of, 22
Bellows, William, 115
Benin, Bight of, 130, 136, 139
Berry, Claude, 96, 97, 98
Best, Mr, 50, 51, 52, 53, 55

Bideford, 11
Bingham, Capt, 25
Birmingham, 102, 107, 115, 118, 119, 121, 123, 124, 127, 128
Bligh, Capt, 44
Boconnoc, 19, 20-55, 74
Bodmin, 22, 58
Bool, Richard, 108
Borlase, Dr, 90
Bonaventure, Thomasine, 15
Boscastle, 15
Boswell, James, 34
Botallack Mine, 158
Bounty, 44
Bracegirdle, Mrs, 26, 27, 28, 29
Braddon, Lawrence, 15
Bradock Down, 20
Brazen, 137, 139, 140, 142, 145, 155
Brazils, the, 87
Brea River, 165
Bristol, 87, 117, 140
Bristol Channel, 11
British Friend, 121
Browne, Mrs, 27, 28
Bruges, 66
Brunel, Isambard, 101, 118, 126, 127, 128
Brunton, William junior, 119, 120, 121
Brunton, William senior, 118, 119
Buckingham, Marquis of, 21
Budd, Edward, 93, 94, 95, 96, 97
Bulkeley, Viscountess, 85
Bullock, Edward, 93, 94, 95, 96, 97
Burke, Sir Bernard, 25
Burritt, Elihu, 115
Byron, Lord, 15

174 *The Living Breath of Cornwall*

Calais, 57
Callender, 38, 39, 40, 41
Camborne, 102, 106, 108, 111, 114, 160
Camden, 19
Camel, River, 18, 19
Camelford, 19, 79
Camelford, Lord (2nd), 19, 20-55
Campion, Edmund, 62, 75
Canada, 135
Canary Islands, 41
Cape, the, 41, 42, 44
Cape Verde Islands, 140
Carew, 19
Carminow family, 21, 23
Carn Brea, 90, 105
Casson, Sir Hugh, 103
Caxton, 91, 92
Channel, English, 41, 65
Channel Pilot, 76
Channey, Maurice, 66
Charles I, King, 21, 22, 23
Charles II, King, 23
Charlestown, 87, 88
Chatham, 44
Cheshire, 98
Chick, the, 129
Clapperton, Capt Hugh, 131-156
Cleveland, Duchess of, 21
Clovelly, 11
Cockburn, James, 53
Cockburne, Rev W., 47
Colebrook, Major, 135
Collingwood, Adm, 80, 81, 83
Collins, Wilkie, 158
Columbus, 137
Cook, Capt, 44
Cork, 77
Cornwall Gazette and Falmouth Packet, see *Royal Cornwall Gazette*
Courier, 95
Courtenay, Sir Hugh, 22
Courtenay family, 21, 22
Craven, Lord, 27
Cromwell, Oliver, 113
Cumberland, 86

Dagnoo, 148

Daily Chronicle, 124
Daniel, Billy 118
Dawson, Mr, 149
De Cancia, family, 22
Denham, Major, 131, 137
Denmark, 60
Devon, 11, 24, 65
Devonport, 119
Dickson, Dr, 137
Dingley, Mrs, 33
Discovery, 44, 45, 46
Dolcoath mine, 105, 124, 161, 162
Douai, 58, 59, 61, 62, 70, 71, 75
Dover, 51
Drew, Samuel, 20, 23
Drew, William, 24
Dunstanville, Lord de, 90

Edward VI, King, 91
Elizabeth I, Queen, 21, 58, 59, 60, 68, 69, 71, 73
English Social History, 91
Erato, 77
Esk, 156
Essex, Earl of, 22, 23
Euryalus, 82
Exeter, 84, 86, 92, 93, 94, 133
Exeter, Bishop of, 65, 68

Fal River, 101
Falmouth, 78, 80, 82, 83, 87, 88, 95, 101, 129, 137, 167
Family Cruise, A, 123
Fernando Po, 157
Fistral Beach, 129
Flindell, Thomas, 76-99
Ford, Thomas, 62
Fortescue, family, 20
Fowey, 21, 87, 88
Fox, Barclay, 133, 140
Fox family, 137
Fox, George Croker, 137
France, 35, 36, 39, 64, 140
Franklin, Sir John, 120
French Revolution, 39, 57

Gascoigne, Sir Bernard, 23
Gibraltar, 38, 135

Gillet, Louisa, 90
Gillet, Thomas R, 89
Gladstone, William, 91
Glasgow, 123
Glendorgal, 100
Golden, 65, 66, 67, 69, 74
Goldsmith, Oliver, 34
Goulston, 61
Grampound, 22, 95
Great Eastern, 102, 126
Grenville, Annette, 36, 53, 55
Grenville, Sir Bevill, 15
Grenville, Sir Richard, 15, 22, 66, 67, 68
Grenville, Lord, 51, 53
Guardian, 38, 41, 42, 43

Half-Mad Lord, the, 47
Hamilton, Colonel John, 31, 32
Hamilton, Duke of, 25, 30, 31, 32, 33
Hanbury-Tenison, Robin, 157
Hannibal, 141
Hardy, Thomas, 15
Harris, Jane, 165
Harris, John, 158-167
Hartland Point, 13, 14
Harwich, 43
Hawaii, 46
Hawke, 40
Hayle, 88, 90, 106, 117, 119
Heard, Edward, 98
Heard, Elizabeth, 98
Heard, John, 76-99
Henry III, King, 22
Henry VIII, King, 73
Hill, Captain Richard, 25, 26, 27, 28, 29, 30
Historical Discourses of Sir Edward Walker, 23
History of Queen Anne, 30
Hodbarrow Miner, 56, 101
Hodgkin, Eliot, 121
Holland, 32, 140
Holland, Lord, 54
Holywell, 129
Hooper, William, 96
Houtson, Mr, 145, 146, 148, 149, 150
Howe, Lord, 38

Humba, 148

Illogan, 100, 102, 106, 113, 114, 119, 125, 128
India, 46, 126

James, Henry, 96
James, Miss, 86
James Stephens 5, 101
Jansen, Cornelius, 21
Jeffreys, Judge, 57, 72
Jenkin, Alfred, 103, 109
Jenkin, Hamilton, 103, 104
Jenkin, William, 103, 104, 105
Johnson, Dr, 34
Journal of the Night 1832, 133
Journal of the Reign of George III, 35
Juliana, 77

Kano, 151
Katunga, 149
Keisl, Mary Ann, 109
Kemble, Fanny, 15
Kempenfelt, Admiral, 40, 41
Kennedy, Lord, 25
Kensington, 19, 31
King, Lt Philip, 41
Kingsley, Mary, 138
Kingsley, Henry 140
Knox, Thomas Francis, 58, 59

Lake, 23, 36
Lander, Richard, 129-157
Land's End, 12, 13, 14, 101, 158, 167
Lander, John, 156
Lanherne manor house, 57, 75
Lanhydrock, 103, 105
Lapontière, Lt, 80, 81, 82
Launceston, 41, 68, 69, 72, 75
Leeward Islands, 87
Lely, Sir Peter, 21
Lemon, Colonel, 134
Lerrin, River, 21
Leviathan, see *Great Eastern*,
Lisbon, 87
Liskeard, 19, 20, 22
Liverpool, 77, 133, 140
London, 32, 83, 86, 125

London Gazette Extraordinary, 80, 81, 83
Looe, 83
Lostwithiel, 22
Louis XV, 36
Lusitania, 126
Lusty Glaze beach, 129
Lyson family, 22

Macartney, General, 31, 32
Macclesfield, Earl of, 24, 30
Madeira Islands, 139
Madras, 35
Malpass, 101
Manwaring, Thomas, 24
Manwood, Sir Roger, 71
Maria, 156
Mark, King, 17
Martin, Gregory, 62, 75
Mary, Queen, 60
Massey, J., Hon, 85
Mauretania, 101
Mawgan Porth, 56, 57, 76, 101
Mayne, St Cuthbert, 56-75
Mayne, William, 125
Middleton, Dorothy, 138
Milford, 133
Minorca, 38
Mohun, Lady Charlotte, 24
Mohun, Lord (Charles), 19, 20, 21, 23, 24, 25, 26, 27, 28, 29, 30, 31, 32, 35
Mohun, Lord (John) 22, 23
Mohun, Penelope, 22
Mohun, Sir Reginald, 21, 22, 74
Mohun, Sir Reynold, 24
Mohun, Sir William, 22
Mordred, 19
Morning Chronicle, 95
Morris, John, 59, 72
Morrison, Dr, 137, 146, 148, 149
Moscow, 84
Mountford, Mr, 26, 27, 28, 29
Murray, John, 54

Napoleon, 36, 47, 81, 84
Naval Side of British History, The, 38
Nelson, Lord, 80, 81, 82
Nettleton Junior P., 84, 85

Neuchatel, 37
Newport, 77
Newquay, 76, 78, 100, 101, 129
News from Cornwall, 103
Newton, Isaac, 142
Newton, Rev John, 142
Niger, River, 132, 135, 136, 137, 156, 157
Norden, John, 16, 17
Norway, 60
Nun Cove, 129
Nun, River, 156

Oglethorpe, General, 34
Oldfield, R.A. K., 133, 138, 139
Orleans, Duke of, 35
Ottey, Mr, 53, 54
Oxford, 61, 62, 75

Pacific Ocean, 41, 44, 46
Packenham, Captain, 46
Padstow, 18, 19, 87, 88
Page, Mr, 27, 28
Paris, 84
Park, 131
Parochial History, 23
Pasko, 137
Payne, John, 65
Pearce, RN, Captain, 137, 146, 148, 149, 150
Pearce, Mr, 86
Penhale, 129
Penzance, 68, 87, 88
Pernambuco, 140
Perranporth, 145
Philip of spain, 59
Phillips, Capt, 141
Pickle, 80, 82
Pitt, Thomas (Governor), 21, 35, 36
Pitt, William, 21, 35, 39
Plymouth, 38, 82, 87, 88, 92, 93, 121
Pool, 118
Polwhele, 79
Pope, the, 68, 69, 70, 73, 74
Popham, Sir John, 69
Port Gaverne, 18
Port Isaac, 18
Port Quin, 18

Porth Bay, 100
Porth Joke, 129
Porto Santo, 139
Portreath, 106, 119, 161
Portsmouth, 40, 135, 139, 156
Portugal, 140
Potts, Mr, 89
Powell, Mr, 26
Prague, 75
Prince of Orange, 43
Probus, 65

Quarterly Review, 126
Quiberon Bay, Battle of, 40

Rambles Beyond Railways, 158
Rawe, Richard, 75
Records of Captain Clapperton's Expedition to Africa, 134
Redruth, 90, 100, 102, 104, 106, 108, 110, 114, 115, 119, 120, 160
Resistance, 46
Revenge, 66
Reynolds, Sir Joshua, 21
Riou, Captain, 41, 42, 43
Ripper, John, 119
Romance of the Artistocracy, 26
Ritchie, 131
Rome, 68, 69, 70, 71
Royal Cornwall Gazette, 52, 54, 55, 79-99
Royal George, 40
Runcorn, 56
Rundell, Samuel and Sarah, 108
Russell, Lord, 22

St Agnes, 129
St Austell, 20
St Clement, 90
St Columb, 106
St Ives, 87, 113, 118, 119
St Juliot, 15
St Mawes, 95
Saltash, 79
San Domengo, 134
Santa Cruz, 41, 139
Santissima Trinidada, 81
Say and Sele, Dowager Lady, 85

Scilly Isles, 87, 88
Scobell, Mr, MP, 25
Scotland, 152
Second World War, 68
Sheers, James, 54
Shelley, Percy, Bysshe, 15
Sherborne Mercury, 79, 80, 81, 92
Sherwell, 61
Shobel, F., 85, 88
Sidcot, 115, 116, 121
Simmons, Mrs, 50
Simmon's Bay, 135
Smythe, Rodney Warrington, 129
Sokoto, 136, 151
Somerset, Lord F., 86
Spain, 68, 135, 140
Spray, 11, 12, 14, 15, 17, 18, 56, 57, 76, 77, 100, 129, 145, 158, 159, 167
Stepper Point, 18
Stowe, 15, 66
Sweden, 60
Swindon, 93
Swift, Jonathan, 33
Switzerland, 37
Symmonds, Mr, 97

Tahiti, 44
Tales of Old Travel, 140
Tamar River, 19
Tangye, Alice, 107
Tangye, Anne, 107, 108, 109, 110, 111, 112, 116
Tangye, Edward, 105, 107
Tangye, George, 104, 107, 109, 110, 111, 113, 114, 115, 120, 121, 122, 123, 124
Tangye, James, 105, 107, 114, 118, 119, 120, 123, 125, 127, 182
Tangye, John, 104, 107, 109, 110
Tangye, Joseph, 104, 105, 106, 107, 109, 110
Tangye, Joseph (junior) 105, 107, 114, 117, 120, 123, 125, 127
Tangye, Richard, 102, 105, 107, 109, 110, 112, 113, 114, 115, 116, 117, 121, 123, 124, 125, 128
Tangye, Sarah, 107
Tangye, William, 124

Teneriffe, 139
Tewkesbury, battle of, 22
Thames, River, 126
Thomas, Joseph, 96, 98
Thompson, Surgeon, 54
Times, The, 84, 95
Tintagel, 16, 17
Tobago, 38
Tolstoy, Nikolai, 47
Torkin, 24
Torquay, 77
Towan Head, 129
Trafalgar, Battle of, 47, 80
Tredham, Colonel, 26
Tregian, Francis, 65, 67, 68, 70, 74
Tregony, 58, 74, 79
Trelawny, Edward, 15
Trevelyan, G M., 91
Trevelgue Island, 100
Trevose Head, 76, 77
Tripoli, 135
Tristan and Isolde, 17
Troon, 160
Troubles of our Catholic Forefathers, 59
Truro, 56, 65, 79, 80, 81, 85, 86, 87, 88, 92, 93, 95, 96, 108, 130, 131, 134, 136, 146, 150, 156

Vancouver, Capt George, 44, 45, 46, 47
Victorian Lady Travellers, 138
Victory, 82

Villeneuve, Adm, 82, 83
Vivian, H. H., 85
Voyage into Cornwall's Past, 15

Wadebridge, 58, 75
Wagner, Richard, 16
Walpole, Horace, 35
Warren, Sir George, 85
Warrington, Col, 135
Warwick, Earl of, 30
Watergate Beach, 129
West Briton, 78, 84, 92, 93, 94, 95, 96, 97, 98, 99
West Indies, 79, 87, 134, 135, 137, 141
Western Luminary 84, 94
Western Morning News, 99
Weekly News, 92
Whipsiderry, 129
Wilkins, Edward, 118
William IV, King, 157
Williams, John, 118
Williams, John (merchant) 125, 128
Willoughby, George, 118
Willyams, Humphrey, 130
Wilson, G., 21
Wintour, Edward, 90
Wordsell, Thomas, 121, 122, 123, 124

Yorkshire, Post, 102